"**The Day the Whistles Cried** masterfully braids historical fact with craftily voiced dialog in order to present a story that will wrangle the heart and long impress itself on the mind. Betsy Thorpe is a researcher and front porch storyteller who meticulously interrogates and honors the 1918 Dutchman's Curve train wreck. Its complicated threads of cause, effect, and stunning humanity are rendered in this book that will find itself in the company of important railroad, World War I, and southern culture history."

Named one of *Essence Magazine*'s favorite poets in 2010, Stephanie Pruitt is the editor of a book of poetry, *Regarding Rule 99.*

/

The Day the Whistles Cried

Cornfield Meet

slang

a head-on collision of two train locomotives

The set of railroad tracks known as "Dutchman's Curve" was named after a crew of German rock-cutters. In the 1850s, the workers had been brought to Nashville specifically to help build a railroad leading to the west. Confusing *Deutchmen* for *Dutchmen*, locals named the tracks in their honor—and the name stuck.

The Day the Whistles Cried

The Great Cornfield Meet at Dutchman's Curve

The Story of America's Deadliest Train Wreck

By

Betsy Thorpe

Some descriptions of the wreck and its immediate aftermath featured in Chapter Six, are adapted from eye witness accounts that appeared in the *Nashville Tennessean*, July 10th 1918.

Certain sentences in the Conclusion are adapted from *The Dixie Line*, by Dr. Jesse Burt and are used with permission.

Ideas into Books® WESTVIEW
P.O. Box 605
Kingston Springs, Tennessee 37082
www.ideasintobooks.net

ISBN 978-1-62880-040-1
Second Edition October 2014

Editing by Tracy Lucas
Cover by Paula Underwood Winters
Digitally printed in the United States of America on acid free paper.

Dedication

To my departed husband Peter; I miss you so much. I wish you were here. Always.

ॐ

To Daniel Timmons, Douglas Bates, Willis Farris, and all the other ghosts of Dutchman's Curve; thank you for choosing me to uncover your sorrowful tale. I was honored to meet you. I answered your cries and did as you asked.

My only regret is that I couldn't tell all of your stories in the pages of this book.

May you all rest in eternal peace.

In Recognition

I first met Chris Lambos over a cup a coffee at Shoney's Restaurant just a few days after I learned about the train wreck at Dutchman's Curve. Teresa Cline, my fellow waitress and our mutual friend, brought us together. She'd caught my passion for the train wreck story, and knew that Chris would be enthusiastic for it, too.

Chris is a Nashville native, and he has lived near Dutchman's Curve most of his life. He started telling me what he knew about the area right away. It didn't take us long to figure out that there is something special about the place where the wreck happened, and for the past six years, Chris has guided me along as we worked together discovering and documenting the history and geography of Dutchman's Curve.

Chris Lambos also happens to be a real estate agent. He listens to classic rock-and-roll, has a passion for cool old cars, shares my interest in preserving historic buildings and structures, and is the executive producer of a yet-to-be-titled documentary about the train wreck at Dutchman's Curve.

Acknowledgements

Senator Douglas Henry supported my quest to uncover and preserve this story long before I knew I was going to write a book. He is a true friend of history.

Thank you Senator Henry.

⤳

From the earliest days of this project, my one-time boss Juan Gipson, along with my co-workers and long-time customers at Shoney's Restaurant in Bellevue, Tennessee, provided resources to aid in my research. Their interest in this story never wavered and their encouragement kept me going.

Thank you one and all.

⤳

The Day the Whistles Cried would never have happened without the guidance of my globe-trotting writing guru, Wendy Goldman Rohm. She helped me discover the heart of this story.

Thank you Wendy, I hope I made you proud.

Special Thanks

When I first started researching this book seven years ago, it took no time for Nashville's community of archivists and historians to embrace my project. The story of the train wreck at Dutchman's Curve is one of the biggest stories to come out of Nashville, and they were all happy to help with my research.

I want to specifically thank (the now-retired) Debi Oser Cox of Metro Archives, Sister Marian Sartain O.P. Secretary General, at Saint Cecelia's Congregation, Jay Richiuso, Anita Coursey and Charles Nelson at the Tennessee State Library and Archives, Beth Odle in Special Collection Division at the Nashville Public Library, Barbara Baltz of the Archives of the Catholic Diocese of Nashville, and the late Annette Rankin of the Gordon Jewish Community Center Library and Archives.

I also want to thank Tara Melnik of the Metro Historic Commission, Evelyn Underwood Miles, Dolly Carter, and Paula Allen of the Bellevue Harpeth Historic Association and Linda Knight, of the Tennessee Supreme Court Historical Society. Tara, we didn't know it then, but this book was born the day I called to ask where the train wreck historical marker was. Your response—that there wasn't one, and that maybe I should lead the effort to establish one—set me on an adventure that resulted in this book. Evelyn, Dolly, and Paula, thank you for giving me a base to work from. Being part of the Bellevue Harpeth Historic Association gave me credibility. Linda, thank you for finding the United States Supreme Court decision in the case of JAMES C. DAVIS, AGENT, v. MRS. MARY KENNEDY, ADMINISTRATRIX, ETC. Because of you and your discovery I was able to present the correct and proper conclusion to Mary Kennedy's story.

Last but not least, I want to mention Terry Coats, President of the Nashville Chattanooga Preservation Society. When I first met Terry, I didn't know anything about trains or railroads. One of the first questions I asked him was why there wasn't a caboose on the back of either one of the wrecked trains. He kindly explained to me that a caboose only belongs on the back of a freight train. One will never find one at the back of a passenger train. Ever since that day, he has been my go-to guy on all things railroad, and has on more than one occasion prevented me from figuratively hitching a caboose to the back of my passenger train.

With Profound Appreciation

One evening in 2010, I really hit the research jackpot. That's when I tracked down retired U.S. Department of Labor Historian Judson MacLaury on Facebook. Mr. MacLaury had referenced a 1918 government speech titled "Labor and Victory" in a paper he delivered to the Society for History in the Federal Government in 2000. I discovered his paper in 2008, and tried hard for the next two years to confirm the speech's existence so I could read it in its entirety.

When I finally made contact with Mr. MacLaury, he graciously directed me to an online historic publication, *The Department of Labor: the Negro at Work During the World War and Reconstruction* That book was an invaluable resource to me, one I turned to often while writing about the newly hired Dupont Powder Plant workers killed in the train wreck. During our one and only conversation, Mr. MacLaury encouraged me to revive the vibrant words of the long-forgotten speech.

Thank you, Mr. MacLaury, for sharing your knowledge of the "Labor and Victory" speech with me and the sage advice you gave me on how I should treat its text.

Another "Research Jackpot" was Beth Howse. Ms. Howse was the Special Collections Reference Librarian at Fisk University. She passed away September 26th, 2012, just two days after her sixty-ninth birthday.

It is my great regret that I didn't get to tell her how profoundly my writing of this book was shaped by our discovery of Prince Mysteria's article in the *Chicago Defender*, and that she'll never know how much it influenced my exploration of the World War I African-American experience for the pages of this book. She died before I finished writing it.

When I first met Ms. Howse, I knew very little about how to conduct historical research, yet she treated me like I was a visiting scholar. Once I explained the nature of the event I was researching and what I hoped to find, she brought boxes of materials for me to go through. It was *her* idea that we look through the *Chicago Defender* to see how the leading African-American paper of the times covered the train wreck. She showed me how to use the microfilm reader and was literally standing next to me when I scrolled through pages of the July 1918 issue of the newspaper. She shared my excitement when the words of Prince Mysteria emerged on the screen. We both knew, at that moment, that we had found something immensely important and special: the only known African-American eyewitness account of the train wreck at Dutchman's Curve.

Beth Howse was a joy to be around, and I can only imagine how excited she would be to see this book in print.

Rest in peace, Ms. Howse. May your legacy live on in the work of all the laymen, students, and scholars you have helped along the way.

To My Family and Friends

Mom, recalling that you rode a train all the way from Oregon to Tennessee to help me commemorate the ninetieth anniversary of the worst train wreck in U.S. history still makes me smile.

Geraldine, your enthusiasm for this book makes me happy.

Ruby, thank you for relieving me of my household chores so I could spend more time writing.

Adriana, Tyria, and Mary, you girls will never know how much I appreciated those rare moments of peace and quiet you gave me.

To my longtime friend Annie, I remember the day we sat in your garden. You let me ramble on about a train wreck. Thank you for listening.

John, Joel, Christopher, and Chris, you each helped me so much. In so many ways. Thank you.

Ina, thank you for giving me time off from my job at Shoney's so I could finish writing this book. I still owe you a few shifts.

Cyndea and Kim, finding two new lifetime friends was an unexpected bonus to my research. I couldn't have done this without either of you.

Cara, thank you for always taking the time to answer my random questions about grammar, and for showing me how to put a book together.

Tracy, you turned my rough draft manuscript into a readable book. I am lucky you agreed to work with me. Thank you, my friend.

Paula, from beginning to end, you have encouraged me every step of the way.

Jerry Stringfellow. You were such a good friend to Peter and me. For years we relied on your technical support. Now you are gone and I wish you were here to see this book published—because then you would still be here, enjoying life with your wife and family.

Couldn't Have Done It Without My Backers

In this age of social media, things that were once seemingly impossible are now suddenly things that can actually happen. When I first started writing this book, I wondered how in the world I was going to come up with the money to pay for my publishing costs. It was a worry that was never far from my mind. Thanks to a successful crowdfunding campaign on Kickstarter.com, I was able to raise the necessary amount of money in fewer than thirty days in the fall of 2013.

Listed below are the names of my Kickstarter backers. Because of them, the book once only in my mind is something you can now hold in your hands as tangible reality. There are no words to properly express my gratitude.

~

My Family
   Members:
Nan Cross Mother
Ruby Thorpe
   Daughter
Randy Cross
   Brother
Gene Roe Uncle
Pat Couturier
   Aunt

Frank Roe Uncle
Geraldine Roe
   Aunt
Holly Andrade
   Blair Niece
Paul Blair
   Nephew
Debbie Warner
   Cousin

Connie Couturier
   Kelty Cousin
Marlene Couturier
   Culp Cousin
Sherry Roe Carroll
   Cousin
Teresa Fronapel
   Cousin
Melanie Pond
   Cousin

~

ॐ

Carla Harrell Chamberlain, you really do know how to help a fellow sister out! Thank you!

ॐ

Kari Andrews
Judith Bader
Myra Beard
Margaret
    Bedortha
Carole Biondello
Desiree Bradford
Carolyn Carroll
Kat Conners
Lori Conners
Stacy Brady
Eileen Brayman
Judy Bridges
Leah Cannon
Terry & Jane
    Coats
Deborah Cox
Chip & Barbara
    Curley
Jeff Davidson
Shelby Day
Bill & Betty
    Defelice
Duncan Eve III
Carney Farris
Ellen Fleischer
Ann Forshey
Stephanie Pruitt
    Gaines
Angela Gipson
Annie Heron

Cathy M. Hixon
Donna Holbrook
Peggy Holmes
Tommy Holt
Kim Hoover
Rebecca Irwin
    Horn
Jody Johnson
Joel Keller
Phyllis Kraal
Kara Leist
Christopher
    Ludlow
Mary Lynch
Josh May
Walter & Dawn
    McBee
Pat McGee
Evelyn
    Underwood
Miles
Catherine
    Mountcastle
Sam Oliver
Rose Melton
    Patrick
Loretta Pelosi
Lee A. Photoglou
Lara Pressburger
Victoria Quick
Rita Rauba

John & Katy
    Richards
Gordon Roberts
Jay Rogers
Chris Rose
Sara Rutherford
Kathryn
    Ruttencutter
Joby Saad
Shelia Smith
    Sasser
Patricia Seitz
Jeff Sellers
Christopher
    Shumate
Jack & Sue Spence
Kathleen Starnes
Donna Stockie
Faye Thompson
Sheri Weiner
Judy Therrell
Sherry Trout
Sue Trout
Lois Van Hoose
Tanya Van Hoose
Gregory Wells
Deborah Wibrink
Cathy Williams
Paula Underwood
    Winters
Jonathan Wright

ॐ

In Memoriam: Henry Hill

The photo on the front cover of this book was taken by NC&StL Railway photographer Henry Hill on July 9, 1918. His grandson, Henry Hill III, gave me permission to use that photo, along with his grandfather's other photos pictured in this book, when I visited the grandson's home in Huntsville Alabama in 2009.

When Mr. Hill captured images of the wreck with his Graflex Speed Graphic camera in 1918, he had been working for the railway for less than three years. His career as company photographer went on to span the next four decades.

In 1953 a reporter for the employee magazine the *NC&StL Bulletin* had this to say about his long-time co-worker: *Henry has been 'shooting' a camera since 1903. Long ago he quit carrying 'the little bird' that all photographers once carried for us to 'watch.' He couldn't keep in birds—they couldn't stand the pace. Yes sir. Henry gets around. One day might find him in Chattanooga, the next day in Memphis and the following day testifying in court on a branch line where his pictures will constitute the strongest evidence.*

No one has ever calculated the actual time spent by him, during a year, standing on some cold trestle, bridge or passing track tenderly holding his raincoat over his faithful camera while he gets wetter by the hour.

Perhaps no more disappointed look ever appeared on a man's face than upon his when a cloud drifts across the sun just as he is ready to 'snap the streamliner.'

The total time spent must run into months. He produces an average of three hundred negatives for the legal department alone each year.

At the present Henry is doing an excellent job of copying many old and valuable pictures of railroad scenes, prints of which will eventually find a permanent place in our company archives.

In 1957 the Nashville Chattanooga and Saint Louis Railway was absorbed by a merger with the Louisville and Nashville Railroad. Unfortunately many historic NC&StL documents and records, along with thousands of Henry Hill's photographs and negatives, were ordered destroyed by L&N officials immediately following the merger .

Thankfully some of his negatives survived the destruction. They offer a lasting view of the railway's employees, structures, equipment and important events. Some, including the ones found in this book, go all the way back to the Golden Age of railroads.

Henry Hill III passed away in 2013. He was a diligent keeper of his grandfather's legacy and monitored how his photographs were used

Because of him, you can see for yourself some of the carnage his grandfather, NC&StL photographer Henry Hill, witnessed when he arrived on the scene to document what turned out to be the worst train wreck in U.S. history.

In Memoriam: Elizabeth Jonas Jacobs

I interviewed Elizabeth Jonas Jacobs in 2007. She was 101 years of age and was the last known living witness to the Great Cornfield Meet at Dutchman's Curve.

When I met her, she lived in a condo just a few city blocks away from the wreck site. At the age of twelve she visited the site with her aunt, a Red Cross volunteer, who was sent to the scene to retrieve bags of mail, collected after the wreck, and carry them back to the post office in Nashville.

Her first husband, Homer Jonas, was related to Milton Lowenstien, whose story I tell in this book. Milton and Homer were first cousins and it was during my interview with Elizabeth that I first heard the story of Milton and learned of the unlucky set of circumstances that led to his death.

Contents

Dedication v

In Recognition vi

Acknowledgements vii

Special Thanks viii

With Profound Appreciation x

To My Family and Friends xii

Couldn't Have Done It Without My Backers............ xiv

In Memoriam xvi

Preface: A Quick Note on Method xxi

Foreword by David Ewing xxii

Introduction 1

Part I: The Wreck.. 5

Part II: Placing Blame.. 75

Conclusion 203

Appendix A: A List of the Dead 210

Appendix B: Contributed Article by Paul Clements..215

Appendix C: Contributed Article by Terry Coats........220

Appendix D: Contributed Article by Erin Drake........228

Appendix E: Interstate Commerce Commission 232

Appendix F: Supreme Court Decision 242

References 245

About the Author 249

Preface: A Quick Note on Method

This book is a work of creative nonfiction. Though it might be a simpler description, the magnitude of the horror of the wreck would be diminished in the eyes of the reader if I were to call this book a work of fiction.

The genre definition given by *Creative Nonfiction Magazine* explains, "The word 'creative' refers to the use of literary craft, the techniques fiction writers, playwrights, and poets employ to present nonfiction—factually accurate prose about real people and events—in a compelling, vivid, dramatic manner."

That is what I have attempted here in good faith. In order to bring the story the full of force of humanity it deserves, I took only the liberty to create dialogue and minor, everyday actions which help reveal its truth. The timelines, statistics, historical events, and reported scenarios shared within this book are completely factual and have all been thoroughly researched.

Part I of this book reveals the true and documented actions of the day, and includes my imagined dialogue. The dialogue in Part II is adapted from actual court transcripts.

Foreword

By David Ewing

I met Betsy Thorpe when she was researching a day in Nashville so sad and gruesome people should never forget. Many had already forgotten this day and Betsy wanted to find out the story behind the great train wreck at Dutchman's Curve.

Historic markers line the streets of Nashville commemorating famous homes, people and events. Ninety years after the crash the marker to the train wreck at Dutchman's Curve was dedicated. Betsy had taken this tragic event and memorialized those who lost their lives that day with a marker. She conducted research on who they were and what they did. The events on the ninetieth anniversary of the crash reunited the grandchildren and great grandchildren of those who lived and many who died that day on a horseshoe bend on the railroad tracks just outside the city limits of Nashville. Ninety years later, stories were traded and family memories were shared and Betsy felt this story needed a broader and larger audience.

When most people hear about the worst train crash in American history their first question is *why did it happen*? Betsy in *The Day the Whistles Cried* explores more than those who were killed. She has created a narrative based on the real events of that day, what preceded it and its aftermath. She takes you through a family's struggle as they battle a large railroad in lengthy court proceedings and investigations. The reader has a front seat view of a widow's struggle to receive her husband's railroad pension and of what really happened when two massive steam locomotives crashed at full impact that day.

It's hard to imagine witnessing what over thirty thousand people saw when they visited the crash site on July 9, 1918 but Betsy has taken the reader back to that day and time. That morning started with a crash so loud people from over a mile away rushed to the site. This book takes you back to those times during World War I in Nashville with the employees of the railroad and others on board and how their lives changed in a second.

This book is a masterpiece and is a must read for anyone interested in this tragic event and its aftermath and how it changed how railroads operate today.

⁓

David Ewing is a ninth generation Nashvillian and is the direct descendant of Prince Albert Ewing, the first African American to practice law in Tennessee and a six time judge. David is a Nashville lawyer and is a collector of local African American history and culture.

"Dutchman's Curve" Historical Marker, Nashville Tennessee

Introduction

July 9th, 2008 was my big day. It was the ninetieth anniversary of the worst train wreck in U.S. history. It was also the day that the Dutchman's Curve Train Wreck marker, Metro Nashville Historical Marker #128, was dedicated.

I'd worked for more than a year to have the marker erected, and had arrived at the site early that morning to prepare. Establishing a historical marker is an unusual achievement, especially for someone like me, and as I lingered near the marker, I read the words stamped in granite and reflected on the journey that brought me to that day.

I've earned my share of titles throughout the course of my life: daughter, sister, hippie, wife, mommy, waitress, grandma, and widow are all nouns which have been used to describe me. I gained those names naturally. Each evolved from the ones that came before, and I recognized myself in each of them.

But that morning, as I anxiously waited for the ceremony to begin, I learned that I'd earned a new title, a name that was unrelated to any persona I'd ever used. I first heard it when a young man called out to me. He was a newspaper reporter from Memphis, and he took me by surprise. I must have been thinking quickly that morning, because it took less than a moment for me to respond and step into my new identity. *What the heck*, I thought, as I reached out to shake his hand. "Yes, I'm Betsy Thorpe, the Train Wreck Lady, and I'll be happy to talk to you about Dutchman's Curve."

Whenever I'm asked about the train wreck, I like to begin by explaining that to me, the story is more than the tale of two steam locomotives colliding head-on in a West Nashville cornfield. The story encompasses the history of a specific place. It opens long before events on the 1918 home front propelled wartime efforts into action and set the stage for the accident to occur. It starts even before the early days of railroading, when the set of tracks known as Dutchman's Curve were first laid. The story goes back to the beginning of Nashville's recorded history. The story is fluid. It moves forward, across time. It flows through the day of the wreck, on past the immediate aftermath, and through the years that followed. The story spans the decades between then and now, and includes the present as it continues to unfold before me.

I first learned of the train wreck while reading a book about the history of my Nashville neighborhood. It wasn't unusual for me to be reading up on local history; I have a keen interest in past events, and I've investigated the history of just about every community I've ever lived in. When I walk through the streets of my neighborhood, I want to know who walked there before me. I want to follow their ghostly footsteps and wander through the world they knew.

I was about nine years old when I discovered my affinity for people and times long gone. One day during the summer of 1964, my grandma and I hiked to an abandoned house to dig for glass bottles and other antique treasures. It was the first time she'd taken me up the mountain, and we left right after breakfast, leaving my two brothers and all my boy cousins behind. At that time, my grandparents lived in a ramshackle house on Hard Scrabble Road, a tarred thoroughfare that wound through a forested valley, just a few miles past the logging town of Drain, Oregon.

It took us more than an hour to reach the abandoned house that morning, and as we made our steep climb, my grandma told me stories about the people who once lived there. My grandparents' landlord, ole Mr. Haines, was a widow-man. His late wife, ole Mrs. Haines, had been born in the house, and the land my grandparents' house now sat on and stretches of Hard Scrabble Road were once part of her family homestead. My grandma knew how to spin a tale, and by the time we reached the first fallen outbuilding and passed the remnants of a hay barn, my imagination was alive and I could see the place as a working farm, the way it was when Mrs. Haines was a little girl.

Looking back on that day, I can now say that I think my grandma was a little envious of her. Mrs. Haines had lived her life out on her family home place, and when she died, she was buried in a plot near her people. Like Mrs. Haines, my grandma was also born on a homestead, but hers was in Kentucky, and her Papa took her from there when she was a little girl. Although she descended from one of western Kentucky's earliest settler families, she spent the next two decades moving around between Kentucky, Missouri, and Mississippi. During that time, she married my grandfather. It was right after the birth of their sixth child, and after spending years as Mississippi sharecroppers, that my grandparents moved their family out west. They followed two of my grandma's younger brothers all the way to Oregon where they'd settled after completing duty there with Roosevelt's Civilian Conservation Corps. My grandma spent the rest of her days in Oregon, and although she enjoyed a good life there, she never forgot her childhood home. I believe she always wished her Papa had never taken her out of Kentucky.

I don't remember for sure what all my grandma said that morning as we followed a set of wagon ruts up to the house. What I do recall is the hum of bees buzzing around my ears, and that we walked through a patch of brush and discovered an overgrown blackberry thicket. I know that she was telling me something when we stopped to pick a handful of ripe berries, because that's when the history of that mountainside overcame me. Surrounded by briars and lulled by the quiet mountain, my senses followed her voice back through time. I settled into a new awareness, mesmerized by the rhythm of her Southern speech and absorbed in her old-timey expressions.

Ever since that morning on the mountain, I've had an enhanced perception of time. Since that day, my view of most places I've chanced upon have included either an imaginative or a studied peek into its past. It was that day, as I followed my grandma's voice on a journey through the past, that I took my first steps toward Dutchman's Curve.

The book you are about to read is my imaginative and studied look into the facts of July 9th 1918—the day the whistles cried—one of the saddest days that Nashville, Tennessee, has ever seen.

Part One

THE WRECK

"Never before have such scenes been witnessed in this city, and the horror of the day will long remain in the minds and memory of the thousands that viewed the greatest holocaust the South has witnessed in a generation."

The Nashville Banner

July 10, 1918

Chapter One

In the wee hours of July 9, 1918, the moon hung dark in the Nashville sky. It hovered over the fertile fields and lush forests that bordered the banks of Richland Creek. The luminescence of the fireflies had faded with night, and waterfowl cried out, anxious for the first blush of dawn. In the dimness, the steel tracks of the Nashville Chattanooga and St. Louis Railway curved through dense rows of corn, moving away from Nashville on toward Memphis Tennessee and Hickman, Kentucky.

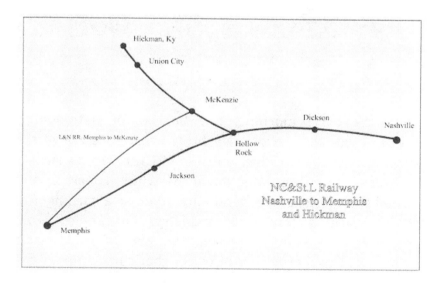

Map Courtesy Terry Coats Collection

High above Richland Creek, Saint Mary's Orphanage perched like a fortress. The orphanage was a sprawling, brick structure with a portal tower at its center. Atop the tower, a stone cross stood high in the dawning sky. Five stories of darkened windows faced the creek, looking out over the winding railroad tracks and the green and yellow fields below. Behind those windows, Dominican Sisters gave the first moments of the day to God, completing the Blessed Sacrament and their private meditations before waking the children for Mass.

Postcard of Saint Mary's Orphanage 1915

In the early morning, few buggies or automobiles moved across the sturdy new bridge that rose above the railroad tracks. The bridge, which in 1913 replaced a rickety old wagon crossing, was made of white concrete and dazzled the eye. The huge landmark stood as a harbinger of the encroaching power of industry. Five miles from downtown Nashville, it marked the end of Dutchman's Curve, that treacherous set of tracks that curved under the bridge and emerged in a straight line on the other side.

၁၃

On this Tuesday morning, Mary Kennedy slept as her husband, railroad engineer David Kennedy, bustled on foot toward Nashville's Union Station with other railroad men and travelers. The eighteen-year-old station was reminiscent of the grand buildings of ancient Rome. Massive gray stone walls and graceful arches supported a high, gabled roofline. A prominent clock tower adorned the front of the structure. A bronze statue of Mercury, the Roman guardian of travelers, soared atop the tower with a winged foot held aloft and one hand raised toward the heavens.

Nashville Union Station, 1918, Courtesy Tennessee State Library and Archives

Kennedy, a vigorous man of seventy-two, was accustomed to walking the dozen city blocks between his home and the station. The electric streetcars that hummed past were of no concern to him; he was muscular, and enjoyed his daily stroll. This morning, he carried a metal railroader's box. The box held a change of clean clothes, work gloves, a Mason jar filled with brewed coffee, and a brass clock.

David Campbell Kennedy, Mary Daughtery Kennedy, 1917, Courtesy Susan Kennedy Gross

David Kennedy was the son of Irish immigrants. He was born and reared on a cotton farm near Tuscaloosa, Alabama, yet he considered Nashville home. He'd settled in the city around 1866 when he first hired onto the railroad.

Kennedy was in good spirits when he arrived at the train shed behind Union Station. The shed was a marvel of modern architecture. It was the largest unsupported structure ever built in America. Constructed of steel, it stood in contrast to the traditional stonework of the adjoining station. The shed stretched five hundred feet behind Union Station and housed numerous railroad repair shops and offices. Its roof covered thirteen sets of railroad tracks and passenger train platforms.

The shed was tucked into a deep gulch, and the only way passengers could reach its boarding areas was by descending the iron stairway from the main lobby inside the station to the platforms below.

Steel beams framed the shed's entrance. Bright rays of sunlight filtered through the beams as Kennedy entered. The morning light cast patterns about the shed, and Kennedy admired the darting display of lights and shadows as he walked through.

Train Shed at Nashville Union Station, 1910,
Courtesy Tennessee State Library and Archives

The railroad operated around the clock, and the night shift was ending as Kennedy headed toward the telegraph office to pick up his train orders. Along the way, he met a crew of off-duty railroad workers headed to the bathhouse. Their overalls were soiled and stiff; their faces streaked with grease. "Don't forget to wash behind your ears, son," Kennedy called out to one young chap.

As Kennedy arrived outside the telegraph office, he saw a group of passengers standing nearby. They were waiting to board Kennedy's train—the Number Four westbound morning train. Amidst the group of passengers were some young military recruits. This morning a group of thirty recruits had hoped to catch the Number Four train, but it was overbooked and only five of them were granted tickets. The remaining twenty-five stayed inside the station to await passage on the next train west, scheduled to depart at 10:00 p.m.

Kennedy glanced at the five recruits. One of the boys playfully tapped the shoulder of the fellow in front of him. The young men reminded him of his son, John George, and he quickly looked away.

Three months prior, Kennedy had quarreled with his son after he'd caught the boy trying to sneak off in the middle of the night. "You can't keep me here." the boy had cried.

Like a true patriarch, he'd leapt at his son with a roar, "I'll not have you staying out all night! You shall go to school tomorrow. 'Tis mine and your mother's wish that you complete your schooling and go on to college. I'll not have you disappointing us."

The next morning, young Kennedy slipped away from the apartment he shared with his parents and two unmarried sisters. He immediately signed on with the cavalry of the 30th Tennessee Division, and was now fighting Germans somewhere in France. He was just sixteen years of age, and his father sorely missed him.

The clamor from the train shed echoed through the office as Kennedy entered. Although the railroad had recently installed telephones in their Nashville offices, the telegraph was still the company's main form of communication. The machine was already whirring, its springs and paddles jiggling and bouncing while the keys clicked out messages and orders. The telegraph operator, busy translating the series of dots and dashes coming through the telegraph, barely acknowledged the engineer's greeting. He busily logged the jumble of incoming communications.

Conductor James Preston "Shorty" Eubank rushed into the office. "You have our orders?" he asked the operator as he hurried in. He turned to Kennedy.

"Cheery morning," Kennedy said.

The two men were old hands on the road, and had worked the morning run to Hickman, Kentucky, together for three years. Eubank grabbed his copy of the orders from the operator and waited impatiently as the operator handed another copy to Kennedy.

"Hurry up and read them orders, Uncle Dave, so we can go on and get out to the train."

Kennedy read the orders out loud. Eubank recited them back, and the two men headed toward the door.

On his way out, Eubank paused, reached inside his vest pocket, and took out his railroad watch. He checked it against the clock hanging on the office wall. The watch was running precisely on railroad time. He put it back into his pocket, dashed out to the tracks, and caught up with Kennedy.

"Looks like we might be late meeting Number Seven at Harding," he said as the two men scurried out to track Number Three.

Chapter Two

Inside the train on track Number Three, Conductor Eubank found George Hall, the colored porter, and read him the train orders. Outside, Kennedy walked down the track toward the locomotive at the front of the train. This morning, the train consisted of one mail and baggage car combination, one baggage car, and six passenger coaches; all were made of wood. Newer passenger trains included cars and coaches made of steel, but this one was old and flimsy. To save money, railroad bosses and stockholders had put off replacing the train for quite some time.

Kennedy continued walking alongside the train while the conductor and the porter hurried through the coaches. They checked to make sure the coaches were tidy.

A water closet sat at the back of each coach. The toilet inside emptied its sewage onto the tracks below. The porter unlatched the door to the water closet inside one of the regular coaches. The closet was dank and smelly. Eubank quickly peered inside. "It looks clean enough, George, latch it back up." The conductor and porter made their way to the next coach.

Outside, Kennedy tipped his cap to the men working on the train. He shook hands with those laboring along the tracks and walked toward his steaming locomotive.

Railroad Porter, George Hall, from the Nashville Globe, July 1918

Engine #282 was a fine machine. Built for the railway in 1906, she was a Baldwin Class 4-6-0. Known as a *ten-wheeler*, she had four leading wheels and six driving wheels. The four leading wheels were designed to support the boiler and help the locomotive negotiate curves. They were small and unpowered. The six heavy, cast-iron driving wheels stood five-and-a-half feet tall. Coupled together with steel drive rods, the wheels were powered by steam-driven pistons. The Baldwin 4-6-0 was a mighty engine able to pull heavy freight

15

trains and fast passenger trains over long distances. It was one of the most popular locomotives on the line.

↫

Inside the locomotive cab of the Number Four, Fireman Luther Meadows worked at steaming up the engine. The power of a steam locomotive was controlled by the fireman working inside its cab and was only limited by the strength of his back. On this morning, Meadows had showed up early to begin his day of laborious duty.

Meadows wore a bandana tied around his neck. While he bent over the hot firebox, he pulled his bandana up over his mouth and nose. The bandana offered scant protection from the coal dust that filled the air, but it did filter out some of the hot particles in the smoke. This prevented him from inhaling the smoldering cinders that erupted in his face when he pitched coal into the firebox.

A short tender carrying coal and water stood behind the locomotive. *NC&StL*, the railway's abbreviation, was sprawled across its side in bold letters. Fourteen thousand tons of coal filled the fuel bunker inside the car. On top of the bunker, a horseshoe-shaped water jacket surrounded the heaping mound of coal. More than three thousand gallons of water flowed from the jacket into the boiler at the front of the locomotive engine. Although the bunker held enough coal to complete the day's journey, the jacket held only one third of the water needed to reach their destination. Two scheduled water stops waited down the road.

Behind the tender, the combination mail and baggage car rested on the tracks. It was the first car on the train, and its door was flung wide open. Near the door, canvas bags bursting with mail cluttered the floor as railroad postal clerks worked over them. The clerks emptied several bags of mail onto the long sorting table at the center of the car.

Their hands were agile; each of the workers could sort six hundred pieces of mail in an hour, a feat the other railroad workers marveled over.

Outside the second car, baggage men rushed to unload the last of the luggage carts, which were set up on oversized wheels and piled high with passengers' belongings.

Nearby, a man talked with the baggage master. He was a local embalmer, and a shrouded casket rested on a freight cart between the two men. The baggage master signed for the casket and motioned to two workers to come over and get the cart. They rolled the cart to the baggage car and shoved the casket inside. Steam in the locomotive boiler hissed and the smoke stacks spewed cinders into the air as the baggage men hurriedly thrust more luggage into the overfilled car.

Further down the tracks, Conductor Eubank stepped out of the train as the last of the luggage was loaded. He looked at the horde of travelers crowded in the boarding area with dismay. He'd been reprimanded by his superiors for not collecting passenger tickets on time. He'd missed doing that on more than one run.

The first scheduled stop was twelve miles down the road, and judging from the number of passengers waiting to board this morning, he would be hard-pressed to collect all their tickets before they arrived there.

Eubank pulled out his watch, cradled it in his palm, and checked the time. He brushed the sleeves of his jacket and smoothed the brim of his peaked conductor's hat. He then looked out into the hectic train shed.

"All aboard!" he bellowed. The Number Four was almost ready to leave.

Chapter Three

George Hall checked the brass buttons lining the front of his frayed porter's jacket and stepped onto the platform in front of the two ladies' cars. As always, the ladies' cars brought up the rear of the train. They were placed at the back to spare white women the filth and heat of the engine, and to shield them from the company of male passengers.

A woman approached the side of the train and took the porter's hand. "Thank you, George," she said. Safely onboard, she shook free of his helping grasp.

George Hall was used to strangers calling him by his first name; railroad porters were almost always called George. That custom had begun around 1867 when railroad car manufacturer George Pullman started hiring former house slaves to work as porters on his sleeper cars. The idea of calling the porters by Pullman's first name came from the old tradition of naming slaves after their owners. Soon, railroad porters working for other companies came to be called George, also.

The name became so associated with railroad porters that in 1904, a wealthy American named George Dulany started The Society for the Prevention of Calling Sleeping Car Porters "George", a group formed "to restore dignity to the name George." Any white man whose given name or surname was George could join, and many well-known men like baseball player George Herman "Babe" Ruth and King George V of England reportedly belonged to the organization.

As George Hall helped more ladies onto the train, he pondered on how unfair it was that colored women were denied the same service and considerations as white women.

Colored women had no choice but to ride in the segregated car at the front of the train. There wasn't a special car designated for their comfort and protection. The porter knew that colored women throughout the South were in the midst of boycotting because of that discrimination. He'd heard accounts of colored women who were buying first class tickets and demanding entrance into the exclusive ladies' car. Many of those daring women ended up in jail, and although he privately sympathized with their cause, he was thankful that none of those disturbances had ever occurred on his train.

⌇

At the head of the train, the locomotive was ready to move. The mixed odor of oil and coal permeated the sooty air, and black smoke billowed out of the exhaust stack as Kennedy entered the cab. Once inside, he removed the clock from his metal box. Although he enjoyed a strong constitution and good health, his eyes were weak. Even with the help of his eyeglasses, the numbers on his railroad watch were blurry; he still carried it in his pocket, but hadn't relied on it for quite some time.

The clock he carried sat inside a hinged frame. Unlatched, the frame opened like a book, revealing a broad-faced clock on one side and a photographic likeness of his wife Mary on the other. He noted that it was almost seven o'clock when he mounted the clock on the dash. Reaching into the pocket of his striped coveralls, he took out a soft rag. He took off his spectacles, waved the smoky air away from his eyes and wiped the glasses, adjusting them to look at Luther Meadows. Kennedy waved a scrap of paper toward the fireman. "I got our orders here," he said, handing the paper over.

"Meet Number Seven at Harding Station to pick up mail," Meadows read aloud. "Number One being hauled by Engine #281 – hold at double tracks until Number One passes."

The engineer leaned out of the locomotive window. At the rear of the train, Conductor Eubank waved his arms in a circular motion, signaling that the train was ready to roll. Kennedy signaled back with an abrupt half-wave. He reached for the whistle pull-cord that swayed across the open window.

From the earliest days of railroads, the lonesome wail of the train whistle symbolized the romance and adventure associated with rail travel. Engineers had come to treat the pull-cord like a musical instrument, learning to blow a range of notes and chords on their train whistles. Many engineers on the NC&StL had styled their own sound for when they were out on the open road. But now, inside the train shed at Union Station, Kennedy followed standard safety rules. He tugged on the cord and released two blasts announcing that his train was on the move.

With one hand on the throttle, Kennedy powered up the engine. The gigantic locomotive slowly coasted over the tracks and the morning train eased out of the station. Outside, a clear blue sky hovered above. Kennedy looked at the brass clock and turned to the fireman working beside him. "We're only running five minutes behind. We have a fine day ahead of us. We can make up that time once we get past Harding."

✒

When the train started to move, George Hall was in the one of the ladies' cars, whisking a lady's cloak with a little straw broom. His work finished there, he headed out the door.

George Hall and Conductor Eubank met at the entrance of one of the regular coaches. Eubank rushed toward him and the porter stepped back to let him pass by. "I sure am busy, George. I should be watching for the Number One to go by, but I only picked up tickets in two coaches. This train is terrible full and I don't have much time to get through the rest of it."

The porter understood why his boss was fretting. Even the lowliest railroader was privy to company scuttlebutt, and he'd heard about Eubank being scolded for not picking up tickets on time – and how he'd been humiliated by it. He also knew how important it was for the conductor to watch for the incoming train. "Don't you worry none about watching for Number One, boss. I'll keep my eyes peeled for her."

"You do that," Eubank said. He turned his back on the porter and collected tickets from the nearest row of passengers.

Leaving his boss behind, the porter crouched down and inched his way through the crowded train. He peered across the top of tattered seats to look out the windows. They were close where the double tracks merged to form one line. Number One was headed in their direction, and if it didn't go by soon, they would have to stop and wait in a place before the double tracks ended until it safely passed by.

✒

It's been said that most of the problems suffered by the railroad in 1918 could be traced back to Kaiser Wilhelm of Germany and all the trouble he was making in Europe. A war had raged over there for quite some time, but little more than a year had passed since the United States entered the conflict. Men and women on the home front were still adjusting to the changes brought on by the war.

One change had wreaked havoc for Conductor Eubank and other railroad men throughout the country. In December 1917, the Interstate Commerce Commission recommended that the government take control of the railroad industry, and that December 26th, President Woodrow Wilson issued a nationalization order. On March 21st, 1918, the Railroad Control Act was signed into law. To help move troops and military material, the act put the entire U.S. railway system under the control of the federal government for the duration of the war. Ever since then, the NC&StL Railway, like most other railroads in the country, hadn't been run correctly. Government agents took over management of the railroads, and passengers and workers alike suffered when changes were made to long-held routes and schedules.

Freight trains carrying war supplies dominated the rails, and passenger trains were delayed because freight trains had the right-of-way on most sections of track. The movement of people had increased, and passenger trains were overbooked. The military mobilized, munitions plants operated around the clock, and servicemen and newly-hired factory workers filled the trains.

Military enlistment also caused problems for Eubank and other NC&StL long-standing employees. Since 1916, more than two hundred and fifty of the company's seasoned workers had enlisted in the army. In 1917, the Selective Service ordered a draft of men between the ages of twenty-one and thirty-one. Many of the railroad's workers were drafted and ultimately replaced by inexperienced men who were either too young or too old to be called to war, and railroad bosses expected the old timers to pick up the new workers' slack.

On this morning, Conductor Eubank had too many responsibilities. It was his duty to supervise the train crew, make sure that train orders were followed, and ensure that railroad safety rules were obeyed. He was also charged with collecting passenger tickets. His train orders had instructed him to watch for the Number One train, but he also had an overcrowded train with many passengers to tend to—and very little time to collect tickets.

Spotting an unfamiliar railroad worker walking, toward him, away from the back of the train, Eubank called out. "Hey! You my new flagman? You Sinclair?" The conductor took a piece of paper out of his vest pocket and rushed toward the young man. "Here's our train orders, read them. Go back out and stand on the platform of the last car. Watch for the Number One train. Don't leave from there again. Not 'til you see that train go by."

Chapter Four

George Hall entered the Jim Crow car, where colored passengers were forced to ride. The car took its name from the system of racist segregation laws that were established soon after slavery ended.

In New Orleans, in 1892, a man named Homer Plessey deliberately broke one of the Jim Crow laws, the Louisiana Separate Car Act, and was arrested while riding in a whites-only car. The entire system of discriminatory laws was then called into question, and in 1896, the United States Supreme Court ruled that segregation was legal, as long as "separate but equal" accommodations were offered to colored passengers.

In spite of that ruling, most colored accommodations were inferior to the ones set apart for whites, and on this train, the Jim Crow Car was the shabbiest and most crowded coach of all. Many seats were missing, and the seats that did remain were beat-up and broken. A number of riders were forced to stand or sit on the floor. Soot from the engine drifted through the car's open windows, and hot air choked the men, women, and children huddled inside.

The car also doubled as the smoking car for white men. With disregard for the comfort of colored passengers, the white men, who had comfortable seats in other coaches, pressed their way into the Jim Crow car. They gathered there to smoke cigars and pipes filled with strong-smelling tobacco.

Making his way to the back of the coach, a weary George Hall found his porter's stool. He sat down, leaned back, and gazed out the window. Looking away from the window for a moment, he surveyed the passengers in the coach and recognized many of the white men standing nearby. One stocky young man, Milton Lowenstein, was a traveling hat-salesman. A well-liked fellow, orphaned at a young age, he lived with his aunt and uncle. His uncle owned the wholesale millinery company that he worked for.

Lowenstein called out to another young man entering the coach. The young man looked across the coach, surprised to see his friend standing there. "Lowenstein! I thought you left last night on the overnighter."

"I was supposed to, but I got caught up in a good card game." A curl of smoke drifted up from Lowenstein's cigar. "Lady Luck was with me, and I stayed at the table."

"What about your uncle? Does he know you missed catching the night train?"

"No. He thinks I left last night. He expects that I will be meeting with some customers today in Kentucky." Lowenstein drew on his cigar. "The shopkeepers there want to order new hats. They are expecting to see me in their shops soon."

"How are you going to explain being so late to them?"

"Once I get there, I'll tell them that the train made me late. I'll blame it on the railroad. The way trains run these days, they'll believe me," he said.

"If they learn you'll be going away to war soon they'll be forgiving. Even if they don't believe your story." He nudged Lowenstein and smiled. "I'm not so sure about your uncle though. I dare say he won't be so understanding."

Lowenstein nodded in agreement and offered his friend a cigar.

"No, thanks." he said, as he covered his mouth and coughed. "It's too smoky in here; I'm going back to my seat." Lowenstein exhaled a puff of smoke and watched his friend leave the coach.

Close to where Lowenstein stood, a group of men surrounded an off-duty railroad engineer named John Nolan. Nolan held a carved pipe in one hand and absently twisted the waxed end of his long mustache between the thumb and forefinger of the other. He was aboard the train for the purpose of driving it back to Nashville the following day.

John and Letitia Nolan, Courtesy Denise Nolan Delurgio

"How's that son of yours?" asked a man standing near him.

"My boy is fine. He wanted to ride with me today, but this is too long a trip for such a wee laddie." The warm cadence of Nolan's voice filled the coach. John Nolan was born in Nashville. His parents were Irish immigrants, and although his speech was slow and measured like most other Southerners, his drawl was tempered by a thick Irish brogue.

"Do you feel like reciting for us?" another man asked. "It's going to be a long day riding on this train and I could use the distraction."

Nolan was a skilled orator known for his Irish sentimentality. "Perhaps," he said. "Let me think on it while I enjoy my pipe."

In a coach near the back of the train Conductor Eubank collected tickets while George Hall remained stationed near the window in the Jim Crow car, Baggage men stood in the open door of the stuffy baggage car, and postal clerks worked inside the combination mail and baggage car.

Up in the locomotive cab, Fireman Luther Meadows perched near the window watching for the Number One to pass. In the engineer's seat, David Kennedy dabbed smoke out of his eyes as he drove the Number Four train, away from Union Station and on toward The Shops.

ॐ

One thing was for certain; folks living around Nashville were proud of the NC&StL Railway. It was the first railroad to operate in the state of Tennessee. They called it "Nashville's Road" even though it ran all the way across the state, up into Kentucky, more than halfway down into Georgia, and over into parts of Alabama. They even took pride in The Shops and in the railroad's sprawling train yard.

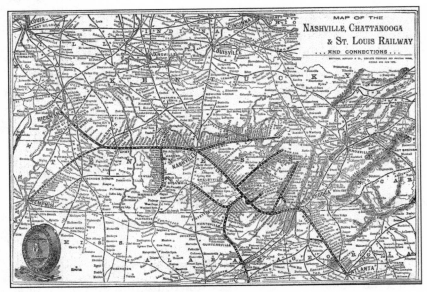

Map Courtesy, Terry Coats Collection

The Shops stood about two miles from Union Station and was located in one of the largest and most important train yards in the South. Most agreed that it was some sight to see. It spread across twenty-three acres and held more than twenty construction, maintenance, and repair shops as well as company offices, the railroad's forty-stall roundhouse, and a giant turntable.

Of all the wonders at The Shops, the turntable with its ninety-foot span and mechanical movements was the most interesting. The turntable served two purposes. The first addressed a troublesome feature of steam locomotives: the fact that their design made it difficult for them to travel in reverse. Oftentimes, a locomotive needed to turn around so it could head out in a new direction, and sometimes when that situation occurred, the locomotive was driven onto a turntable and spun around. The other purpose of the turntable was to help distribute locomotives within the roundhouse stall whenever one needed an overhaul by mechanics.

The mechanics working at The Shops were top notch. Not only could they rebuild an engine; they also knew how to fix a wrecked locomotive and make it run good as new.

Many of the crafts of American industrial society were found at The Shops. Mechanics, carpenters, boilermakers, painters, wheel-makers, machinists, and blacksmiths all worked at The Shops, and most families living nearby boasted at least one worker there. Railroaders started settling in the area around 1875, when the railroad expanded its service west. So many new workers were hired by the railroad at that time that a planned suburban neighborhood, one of the first in the country, was built to house them. The neighborhood turned out to be a fine place to live. It was surrounded by acres of cornfields, and many of its homes overlooked the banks of Richland Creek.

ॐ

As David Kennedy drove his train over a set of tracks that ran through The Shops, another train rolled toward him on a different set of tracks. The train coming toward him from the opposite direction was being hauled by a small switch engine.

A switch engine is a locomotive that transfers empty trains from the train yard where they are stored to the train depot from where they would later depart. This switch engine was pulling an empty ten-car passenger train to the Nashville Union Station.

At the same time and about ten miles down the road, another train, the Number One overnight-express, sped toward Nashville. Hauled by Locomotive #281 and driven by Engineman Bill Lloyd, the overnighter from Memphis was running at full steam. The locomotive was a twelve-year-old engine. Purchased in 1906, she was the identical "twin sister" of #282, the locomotive David Kennedy was driving this morning.

Inside the locomotive cab of the Number One from Memphis, Fireman Thomas Kelley worked beside Engineer Lloyd. Wiping his hands on a balled-up grease rag, he dabbed his sweaty chin. "It's been a long night. I'm ready for the bathhouse," he said. He turned toward Lloyd. "What you plan to do once we get to Nashville? Are you really going to retire? Is this truly your last run?"

Lloyd reached up, grabbed the brim of his cap, and removed it from his head. Holding the cap against his chest, he looked over at the fireman. "You have my solemn word, son. This really is my last run."

Chapter Five

Back at The Shops, Kennedy drove past the switch engine and the train it was hauling as he headed the Number Four toward the semaphore tower up ahead. The semaphore was a wooden tower with two hinged arms. The movable arms were set to display different signals, messages, and warnings. The semaphore was part of a signaling system developed in the early days of railroading, and this one was used to convey information to train engineers proceeding through the yard.

The morning train neared the tower. Inside the locomotive cab, David Kennedy and Luther Meadows noted that the semaphore's arm was pointed up, giving the signal to proceed.

Kennedy nodded toward the set of tracks on which the switch had just passed. "Did you see the train that just passed by? It must've been Number One. Let's get going. Time to pick up the mail at Harding." He blew his train whistle and headed on toward the mainline.

In an office near the semaphore tower, tower operator J.S. Johnson began his new workday as Kennedy piloted his train by. The operator took a sip of warm coffee and looked down at the logbook sprawled across his desk. He logged the time that the morning train passed. According to procedure he picked up the phone and asked the telephone operator to get the Chief Dispatcher at Union Station on the line so he could inform him of Number Four's status.

"Did Number Four pass?" the dispatcher asked.

"Passed."

"Stop him! Number One just passed Bellevue. *Can you stop him?!*" The tower-man slammed his coffee cup down, dropped the phone, and dashed outside. Bellevue Station was about ten miles down a single line of tracks—and the Number Four morning train was about to enter the very same section of track that the Number One overnighter was rushing in on.

Johnson blew the emergency whistle, signaling the train to stop. He scurried down the steps of the tower onto the tracks. The morning train was still in the yard. He desperately looked for the flagman who was supposed to be riding on the platform of the last car, trying to signal him to stop the train. It was the flagman's job to protect the back of the train, but this morning, Number Four's flagman was missing from his post. No one was there to heed the warning.

A group of men stood along the tracks, and the train was about to pass them by. Seeing that the tower operator was trying to stop the train, they started waving their hats in the air, hoping someone on board would see what they were doing and tell the conductor to stop.

Number Four sped away from The Shops, leaving the tower operator and the men standing along the tracks all helplessly watching as it disappeared from sight.

Inside the train, Conductor Eubank hurried to get the fares collected. He only had two more coaches to get through, and he was hopeful he would get through them before they reached Harding Station.

Up in the Jim Crow car, the porter, George Hall sat up straight. His eyes fixed on the scene outside the window. He gasped and jumped off his stool. The train had passed the spot where they were supposed to stop and wait for Number One! They had left the double tracks without waiting for Number One to go by, and now they were out on the main, speeding down the same tracks that the overnighter was coming in on.

Across the car from George Hall, Milton Lowenstein blew smoke rings into the air. The crowd around John Nolan increased as word got out that he was about to recite.

In the baggage car, workers moved away from the open door as the train picked up speed. In the combination car, postal clerks stacked bags of sorted mail by the door.

Up in the cab, Luther Meadows leaned out the window to look at the tracks ahead while Kennedy opened the engine even wider. Coal in the firebox smoldered, water in the boiler bubbled, steam in the engine pushed against the pistons, and the giant locomotive picked up more speed.

Kennedy pulled the whistle cord. The train whistle cried as he opened the throttle wide and rolled across the mainline, and on toward Dutchman's Curve.

‿ᴈ̉ᴏ

While the Number Four train sped into Dutchman's Curve, the Number Seven train sat at Harding Station about three miles away, waiting for the Number One train to pass by. That train had to go by before the Number Four could arrive at Harding Station to pick up the mail Number Seven had collected along its route the night before. Number Seven sat on the tracks facing east toward Nashville.

When the Number Four train usually arrived at Harding, it would slow down. The postal clerks would stand in the open doors of the combination car as the Number Four train passed by Number Seven. Clerks working inside the mail car on the Number Seven train would toss bags of mail from their car into the combination car on Number Four.

Inside the locomotive cab of Number Seven, the engineer pulled off his leather gloves. Tossing them on the seat, he jumped out of the cab and down to the ground. His train orders said to wait at Harding for the Number Four train. He figured Number Four was waiting at The Shops for the Number One. Number One hadn't passed by Harding Station yet, and the engineer reckoned he had about fifteen minutes to while away. He decided to walk around and bide some time.

Harding Station had a little white depot. It had been built by the owners of the Belle Meade Plantation about fifty years prior as a private railroad stop for the plantation's family, guests, workers, and broodmares back when Belle Meade was a world-famous thoroughbred breeding farm. The station was now a whistle stop on the NC&StL Railway line.

Few spots near Nashville were as appealing as the setting around Harding Station on this Tuesday morning. The plantation mansion stood across the road. Trimmed lawns rolled down from its columned porch, and green pastures sprawled beyond. Belle Meade Plantation was well over a hundred years old and had been long admired as one of the loveliest properties around.

Richland Creek streamed between the mansion and Harding Station. Mossy stones and gnarled trees lined its banks. The creek ran alongside a straight line of railroad tracks toward the gleaming bridge ahead. Cornstalks filled the landscape, concealing the tracks as they stretched into the distance, beyond the bridge, and clean out of sight.

ॐ

A couple of miles down the tracks, the Number One train from Memphis barreled toward Harding Station on the way to Nashville. The train was crowded, and an overfilled baggage car rode at its front. Amidst the piles of baggage jammed inside the wooden car, two steamer trunks stood stacked together. The trunks belonged to a group of Dominican Sisters, who taught at the Sacred Heart School in Memphis. They stayed at Sacred Heart during the school year, but the Motherhouse at Saint Cecelia's Convent in Nashville was actually their home. With school out for summer, they planned to spend the next few weeks there. They each owned a spare habit, and those habits lay neatly folded inside the trunks, along with their few personal belongings.

Harding Station, Courtesy Tennessee State Library and Archives

Two Jim Crow cars rode in line behind the baggage car. More than a hundred and twenty-five colored workers from Mississippi, Arkansas, and other rural areas near Memphis crowded inside the two coaches. They'd signed on with the Unites States Employment Service just the morning before.

Most were farmers who, seeing that their fields were in order, had contracted to help manufacture black powder at the newly opened DuPont Company munitions plant near Nashville. Other workers contracted out to the Mason Hanger Company to help complete the construction of the powder plant. They all had signed up to work for only three months so they could get back home in time for fall harvest.

When the United States declared war on Germany, there had been no factories in the country large enough to produce the amount of explosive powder needed to win the war. Finding proper sites to build powder factories began at once. A site near Nashville was selected to build the DuPont Powder Plant, the largest one of all.

The plant and adjoining factory town, designed to be the world's largest powder-factory complex, had started producing explosive powder on July 1st. Although the plant had already shipped its first batch of powder, parts of the factory and much of its town and railroads were still under construction. Once completed, the factory would be capable of producing two hundred and fifty tons of powder a day, and when the town was also completed, it would be able to house a hundred thousand employees.

Workers of all kinds were needed at the DuPont plant and at other factories throughout the country, and there was a nationwide effort to persuade colored farmers to do wartime factory work.

Of all the new hires on the train this morning, nineteen-year-old Matt Toles was among the youngest. A few days earlier, on the Fourth of July, a passionate speaker had delivered a message to men and women gathered at a holiday picnic held near his home in Hernandez, Mississippi.

More than two thousand colored orators were sent out that day to deliver "Labor and Victory," a government-sponsored speech. The orators addressed farmers and other rural workers at patriotic celebrations throughout the South. The speech reached more than a million colored men and women on that afternoon alone. It stressed the role of colored workers in the "world struggle for democracy." Zealous orators shouted the government's call to action: "Negroes are being asked in every city, town, and rural district to join in this work of winning this war. We, like other folk, are having an unusual chance to work and save our country. Let every one of us be wide-awake, and make the most of this opportunity. Let him bear in mind that every time he makes good on his job, he helps his country and the race. Let him also remember that every time a Negro falls down on his job, he pulls down his country and the entire race, and thus makes winning the war less possible."

The closing words of the speech were frightening: "Any person who does not work hard, who lags in any way, is against his country and is, therefore, our bitter enemy."

In these uneasy times of war, nobody cared to be called "enemy," and it was no surprise that so many workers— even young ones like Matt Toles—had signed up the day before to do wartime work in Nashville.

Three more wooden coaches lay between the wooden Jim Crow cars and the two steel-framed sleeper cars at the back of the Number One train coming in from Memphis. Inside the men's sleeper, Monsignor Dennis Murphy drew back the curtain in front of his bunk.

Monsignor Murphy was one of the most respected Catholic clerics in the state of Tennessee, and men of all faiths were inspired by his understanding of scripture. That and the fact that he'd studied theology at the American College in Rome gave him an air of authority over all things holy.

Monsignor Dennis Murphy, Courtesy Nashville Catholic Diocese Archives

As the Monsignor pushed his legs through the curtains, the sound of a loud bump—followed by a rowdy, "Damn!"—erupted from behind another curtained bunk across the aisle. The offender held the crown of his head as he stuck his face through his own curtain.

38

"Holy-Jesus-Joseph-and-Mary, Father. I forgot you were out here. Please forgive me."

Behind the men's sleeper, in the ladies' car, a fifteen year old girl asked the porter to bring her a washbowl so she could rinse her face. Up in the second Jim Crow car, a group of factory workers played dice while other workers slept. In the cab of the locomotive, Engineer Lloyd piloted the train toward Nashville.

Chapter Six

Inside the segregated cars of the Number One train, the powder-plant workers rode under the watch of two DuPont company bosses. In the first car, one of the bosses guarded more than seventy factory hands. The other boss was in charge of the workers riding in the second car.

In the front corner of the first car, three seated women and a child slept. One of the women leaned against the corner wall, and the child stretched his legs across her lap, his head propped on the knees of the woman sleeping next to her. The third woman rested with her hand on the child's chest. The boss looked away. The three women were not listed among his charges, and were of no concern to him.

Pushing his way through the car, the boss made his way to the doorway leading to the second Jim Crow car, entered, and found his work partner. "We're almost to Nashville. It's time to gather the work crews together. "

"I have something here for you," the second boss said. He held a government-issued broadsheet. "Have one of your workers read this out loud to the others," he said. "Bring it back to me once that's done."

Walking back toward the front coach, the boss passed by the group of workers shooting dice. They huddled together in a tight circle.

"Hand me those dice," he barked. "Gambling ain't allowed!"

The men stood up, turned over their dice and moved to the back of the coach as the boss-man returned to the first coach.

Once there, he rattled off the names of some of his charges. Carlton, Faulkner, Hudson, Toles, Woods," The men stepped forward. "Can any of you read?" he asked.

A man raised his hand. "I can, sir."

The boss-man held the broadsheet in his hand. He thrust it at him. "Read this."

He then addressed the whole car, shouting, "This was written by a colored man who knows why so many of you fail. Listen and heed his words."

The man holding the broadsheet cleared his throat. The sound of the train's wheels racing over the tracks filled the coach, and he had to yell to be heard. "WHY HE FAILED! He did not report on time. He watched the clock. He loafed when the boss was not looking. He stayed out with the boys all night. He said, 'I forgot.' He did not show up on Monday and he wanted a holiday every Saturday. He lied when asked for the truth."

The man handed the broadsheet back to the boss-man and moved to the front of the coach. He crowded against the wall with five other powder-plant workers. He faced the corner where the three women rested with the child. The child awoke and cried, stretching his arms into the air. The middle woman lifted him up off her lap. She held him, cradling him in her arms as the overnight train sped toward Harding Station and the looming bridge up ahead.

On the sidetrack at Harding Station, the engineer of Number Seven stood next to his locomotive. A train whistle cried in the near distance. He looked to the west, where the Number One train thundered down the tracks.

Less than a mile away, on the other side of the bridge, David Kennedy drove the Number Four train through Dutchman's Curve. The train rolled furiously toward the bridge, Harding Station, and the oncoming Number One train.

Inside the Jim Crow car on the Number Four, George Hall hurriedly pushed through the crowded coach, trying desperately to get to the door. Conductor Eubank was in one of the coaches on the other side, and he needed to reach him with the news of what Engineer Kennedy had just done and the imminent danger they were all now in.

Eubank would be able to signal Kennedy to make an emergency stop by tugging twice on the emergency whistle cord that ran throughout the train. The whistle would sound up in the locomotive cab. Being just a porter George Hall was forbidden to make such a decision, but Eubank being a conductor had the authority to do so.

Once told, the conductor could also choose to stop the train himself by turning one of the angle cocks found near the valve at the back of every coach. Turning the angle cock released air in the valve, forcing the train to make an abrupt stop. As soon as the train stopped moving, the train crew could run up the tracks and wave down Locomotive #281. They could set up some flags and signal the engineer driving the incoming train to stop likewise.

Pressing past the group surrounding John Nolan, George Hall heard the engineer recite *In Flanders Fields*, a popular poem that most everyone knew.

"We are the Dead. Short days ago we lived, felt dawn, saw sunset glow, loved and were loved…"

At the front of the train, inside the locomotive cab, David Kennedy guided the train through Dutchman's Curve.

Up ahead, the new bridge gleamed. It stood white against the cloudless sky. Kennedy entered the last loop in the bend; the bridge was close. He rounded a bend and the bridge briefly disappeared from sight again. He could see only a few feet down the tracks as he drove through a blind spot on the curve.

Kennedy pulled his rag out of his pocket. He dabbed at the greasy beads of sweat dripping down his forehead as he steered his locomotive around the hill and out of the blind spot.

The bridge was now within sight. A curl of smoke rose above it and darkened the sky. Below the swirling funnel of smoke, another locomotive sped under the bridge, thundering down the tracks toward Kennedy as he roared out of the curve.

Smoke from the two engines mingled in the air as the locomotives faced each other. Black whirls of heat covered the tracks between them.

Kennedy leapt from his stool and jerked the emergency brake. He looked over at Luther Meadows and whispered, "Sweet Mother of Jesus," as the smoke from the locomotive in front of them filled their cab. Kennedy made the sign of the cross across his chest, lifted his arm to cover his face, and leaned back to brace for the crash. He uttered a prayer for the dead as the steel beams framing the head of his engine struck the head of the locomotive in front of him.

One hundred and sixty tons of iron slammed together as the two locomotives crashed into each other, meeting head-on. Burning coals from the fireboxes flew through the cabs as the force of the impact propelled the two steel beasts straight up and into the air. Scalding hot water spilled down to the ground as the boilers ripped off from the driving wheels below. The bubbling cauldrons fell into the cornfield in an explosion of steam and boiling spray.

The locomotives hurtled back down, trapping the men inside. The wooden passenger trains they were hauling wrecked. The baggage car of the Number One train shattered to bits.

The impact of the collision drove the Jim Crow car of the Number Four train straight through the baggage car in front of it. The Jim Crow car smashed through, pinning the men and women inside between the walls of the two cars. The next two cars, both packed to the aisles with passengers, piled high into the air. Bodies flew out.

The coaches from the Number One train derailed into the surrounding cornfields. They smashed into the telephone poles standing alongside the tracks; the poles fell, crashing down on top of the wrecked train.

⁓

The sound of the crash shattered the quiet morning. Upstairs at Saint Mary's Orphanage, a group of children rushed to a window to see what had happened. They'd heard that same sound a few months earlier, on February 2nd, when another deadly train wreck had happened on the tracks outside their door. Three railroad men had died in the fiery collision that day. On this morning, when they looked out onto the gruesome scene below, the children knew something far worse had happened.

The orphans ran outside. One of their guardians, Sister Mary, had already fled the building, and they hurried to catch up with her. They reached her at the crash site. An eerie sight greeted them in the cornfields beyond the wreck. The white tunics and black veils of the Dominican habit fluttered in the field—caught on the cornstalks where they'd landed.

"Look at the garments hanging on the corn!" one little girl cried. "Sister Mary! Whose clothes are those?"

Sister Mary bent down and spoke to the child. "I don't know who they belong to. Don't fret. We'll find out soon enough."

She stood up and gathered the children around her. Shielding the smallest ones from the sight of the wreckage, she reached out to a tall boy. "Take the wee ones back to the orphanage. I will stay here. There's much to do here, and I must help."

She pushed one of the little ones forward. "Go, now." The children left and she rushed across the field to offer aid.

The scene in front of Sister Mary was terrible. From across the wreckage and beneath, shrieks and muffled cries arose, and helpless victims prayed for speedy deliverance or death. The fields near the tracks were littered with fragments of wood and steel, hurled from the demolished cars. Postal bags had erupted inside the combination mail car. Thousands of pieces of mail had burst from the car, filling the air. They filtered down and now lay strewn across the site. Trunks and suitcases had been hurled out of the crashed baggage car. The baggage lay broken and empty on the ground; the belongings they once held lay scattered across the cornfields. Dead bodies and injured people had been thrown from the train. The dead sprawled where they landed, and next to them, the dying writhed in agony. Sister Mary looked around. Everywhere around her were suffering, blood, and chaos.

The following pages of photos are by Henry Hill, official photographer of the Nashville Chattanooga & St. Louis Railway. Courtesy of Henry Hill III.

Others had already arrived when the sister and her wards reached the site. Three motorists had abandoned their cars up on the bridge. They'd run down to the crash and were working with their bare hands to free the victims trapped between the walls of the telescoped cars. With his train crew on board the engineer of the Number Seven had rushed his train out of Harding Station about one mile away. They joined the three motorists. Farmers who'd been working in the nearby fields rushed toward the wreck. They carried hoes and shovels, and they hurried to help. Using their farm tools, they ripped boards away from the outside of the telescoped car.

"Help us Mother Mary, Solace of the Afflicted, pray for us Saint Joseph, Patron of the Dying." Sister Mary prayed out loud as the rescuers yanked a man from between the walls of the two cars. He was barely breathing when they pulled him from where he'd been pinned. She rushed to the side of the dying man, and kneeling down beside him, she held his bloodied hand. The rescue workers pried more planks away from the telescoped cars, and a pile of dead bodies tumbled out of the car. The men pulled more and more bodies out until a line of corpses formed next to the telescoped cars. Sister Mary looked back down at the dying man. She prayed aloud for his soul and watched over him while he took his last breath and died.

Sister Mary stood up and walked away from the spot where the dead bodies lay. She heard the sound of marching feet and looked up to see hundreds of railroad men trooping toward her. With heavy tools slung across their shoulders, they filed by, moving toward the carnage.

"Sweet Jesus, help is here," she whispered.

The men separated, storming directly into the mayhem.

Chapter Seven

NC&StL Company President John Howe Peyton stood in a cornfield near a wrecked railroad car. The car was part of the Number Four train, and although the three cars riding in line behind it had stayed upright and on the tracks in the collision, this car had been knocked off the rails when the accident happened.

The three cars were already gone from the site, hauled away by a locomotive that came from Nashville to get them. Now, that same locomotive pushed a massive wrecker derrick down the tracks to the wreck site. An empty flatcar rode between the locomotive and the derrick.

The wrecker derrick was a huge piece of equipment weighing over a hundred and twenty tons. It contained a gigantic boom and two iron hooks that were capable of lifting railroad cars and sixty-ton locomotives with ease. An operator worked from inside the cab of the derrick.

Upon its arrival, the derrick stopped near the derailed railroad car. John Howe Peyton walked over to its side.

A Shops supervisor emerged from the field next to the tracks. The supervisor was one of the hundreds of men who had marched out from The Shops to help. He joined the railroad president, who listened as he advised him on the best way to clean up the mess so the company could open the tracks back and get trains moving across the rails as soon as possible. Shouting instructions to a work crew, the two men worked together overseeing the job.

Inside the cab of the derrick, the operator slowly turned the crane to face the car. With the crane in place, he lowered the boom. The crew fastened the iron hooks hanging from the boom to the back of the railroad car. Lifting the derailed car off the ground, the operator lowered the boom and placed the car onto the bed of the flatcar.

The workers stepped away as the locomotive started moving, pulling the derrick and the flat car over the tracks back toward Nashville.

By noon, thousands of spectators had arrived at the scene. They crowded onto the bridge to look upon the disaster below. The Number One train stretched down the tracks. Its locomotive and tender lay out of sight, demolished, in a blind spot inside of Dutchman's Curve. The baggage car and the two Jim Crow cars, wrecked and derailed, remained in view. Behind them, one regular coach teetered on the tracks, partially derailed, with the front end of a sleeper rammed up against it. Behind that sleeper, the ladies' car sat steadily on the tracks near the bridge. Its front end had scarcely cleared the bridge when the crash happened, and it was fully visible from above.

The two sleepers sat empty at the back of the train. The cars had suffered little damage in the wreck, and the passengers had cleared out of them soon after the crash. The derailed regular coaches and the two smashed Jim Crow cars held injured and dying passengers trapped inside. Helpers from nearby farms and neighborhoods worked diligently to free them. Many of the volunteers who showed up from the surrounding neighborhoods were family members of men who worked for the railroad.

One railroad worker's wife struggled to help a man who was trapped and suffering inside a Jim Crow car. "Water! I need a drink of water," he cried.

Piles of wreckage separated the two. The housewife held a flask of water in her hand, but she couldn't reach him with it.

"I'll be back to help you," she shouted. "I promise I'll be right back!"

She turned and ran through the cornfield. Stopping at the first house she came to, she borrowed an empty mop bucket and a mop and sprinted back to the man. She poured the flask of water into the bucket and dipped the mop head into the bucket. With water dripping from the dirty mop head, she extended the mop handle across the piles of debris. Shaking the handle, she sprinkled mop water into the man's open and waiting mouth.

Past the two crushed Jim Crow cars, the baggage car lay shattered in the cornfield alongside the tracks. A few yards away, a group of railroad men crouched in front of Locomotive #281. They held their hats in their hands, looking into the smoldering machine that entombed the bodies of Engineer William Lloyd and Fireman Thomas Kelley.

On the other side of the tracks, Monsignor Murphy talked to an embalmer. Surrounded by the remnants of Locomotive # 282, they huddled together near a dead body. The corpse lay under a pile of crumpled iron and splintered wood, and someone had covered its disfigured face with a newspaper before the embalmer arrived.

The embalmer was named William Jones. He clutched a brass clock in his hand. Monsignor Murphy listened carefully as he spoke.

These two photographs are courtesy of The Nashville Public Library, Special Collections

"That's David Kennedy. That's my wife's daddy trapped under that engine." Looking at the body of his dead father-in-law, he whispered, "They said he was still breathing when they found him, but I don't see how." He shook his head and shifted his eyes from the grisly sight.

Jones looked up at the sky. Blue and cloudless, it sprawled in stark contrast to the bloodied ground he stood on. Glancing down again, he examined the brass clock he held in his hand. Lifting it up, he showed it to the priest.

"One of the workers found this in the debris," he said. "It belonged to my father-in-law. The man who found it recognized the picture of my mother-in-law. He just brought it over to me." Taking a deep breath, Jones looked back down at the dead body lying on the ground. "I just saw him at the train station this morning. I'm an embalmer. I was at the station to a ship a dead body. I was signing the casket over to the baggage master when I saw my father-in-law. He didn't see me, and I'm sorry to say I didn't speak up."

"Don't let that burden you none. You had no way of knowing that it was your last chance to speak to him," Monsignor Murphy said. He raised his arms, making the sign of the cross in the air, and prayed over the dead engineer. "*Requiem aeternam dona eis, Domine.* Eternal rest grant unto him, O Lord."

"Curious, isn't it?" Jones said, tugging at the top of his jacket. "He looked to be having a good morning." Pulling on the edge of his collar, he bent his head, wiped the corner of his eye, and looked back up at the priest. "Thank you, Father. It will soothe my wife when she hears that you prayed over her daddy."

Monsignor Murphy patted the grieving man's shoulder. The priest turned and walked away.

Chapter Eight

No one in the sleeper car the priest had been riding in was seriously hurt in the crash. But he was, like many other riders in the car, battered and bruised. He'd been standing and talking to a man in an upper berth when the accident happened. The priest had fallen to the floor when the train suddenly stopped, and the man he was talking to had tumbled down on top of him.

Now, hours after the crash, Monsignor Murphy was in pain, and he limped through the wreck site. Walking through a conglomeration of wood, iron, steel, glass, and human remains, he found a cleared spot and sat down to rest near the tracks.

Down the tracks, a row of mangled bodies lay in the cornfield. A crowd of bystanders stood nearby, hoping to name some of the victims. Many of the bystanders were passengers who were riding onboard the trains when they crashed. Uninjured, they had stayed on the site to lend a hand in helping rescue their fellow passengers. The others were part of the huge crowd that had rushed out from Nashville seeking friends and loved ones thought to have been on the wrecked trains.

"That's Milton Lowenstein over there," one young man called out. "I was with him this morning. I left him just before the crash. We were in the Jim Crow car—we talked

56

for a moment, and then I went back to my seat. It was too smoky in there."

Another man recognized the mangled body of a popular railroad engineer. "That's John Nolan lying over there," he said. "I know his family well." He stopped talking and moved closer to Nolan's body. "His little son sure is going to be heartbroken," he muttered.

Above the row of bodies, four other bodies dressed in military uniforms lay together. Two women, volunteers from the Nashville Chapter of Red Cross, stood above them. It was a newly opened chapter, and this was the first disaster they had been called to respond to.

One woman held a stack of folded American Flags. The other woman knelt down. She reached up for one of the flags. Covering the first body with it, she looked up and said, "These boys just signed on yesterday. They died for their country same as if they had gone over there to Europe and fought."

In silence, she covered the next two bodies. Reaching the last body, she spoke to her companion as she draped the flag over his face and covered his broken limbs. "This boy is only twenty-two years old. I spoke to his mother on the telephone. I promised her I wouldn't leave his side until someone from his family arrives to claim him."

Monsignor Murphy focused his attention to the scene on the other side of the tracks. A group of colored volunteers swarmed around a mound of dead bodies where dozens of victims lay piled together.

One volunteer cried out. "That's my friend!" He reached out with one hand and grabbed the arm of an older man standing next to him. The man held a small notepad and pencil in his hand. Stuffing them into the pocket of his suit jacket, the man embraced the volunteer who grabbed him. The volunteer raised his hand and pointed a finger toward a crushed body lying inside a bloodied railroad porter's suit. "That's him. That's George Hall. I'd hoped he wasn't working aboard the train this morning. I prayed we wouldn't find him here."

The man spoke to the volunteer. "I am sorry about your friend," he said. "Too many of our race is lying dead in this field. Too many of our race was slaughtered here today! This is an outrage!"

Climbing on top of a piece of a shattered railroad car, he took the small notepad out of his pocket. Reading from the notes he had scribbled down earlier in the day, he addressed the volunteers. "Hear me!" Towering above them, he clapped his hands to get their attention.

They dropped their tools and stopped working. Removing their hats, they stood still and quiet as the man quietly spoke. "God works in mysterious ways His wonders to perform. Must we always be penned up in the most dangerous place on the train, where it is impossible to save ourselves in such cases as this?" he asked. "Take heed! Segregation must end! It must end here. It must end now!"

The man looked around. Seeing Monsignor Murphy watching from the other side of the tracks, he stopped talking. A wagon pulled up behind him. Acknowledging the undertaker sitting in the seat of the wagon, the man waved his hand and signaled the volunteers to go back to work.

The undertaker reached into the back of the wagon and picked up a pile of white shrouds. "Wrap the bodies that are whole in these coverings," he said, as he handed them over to one volunteer. "Stack them in my wagon." He lifted out some metal washtubs. "Put the body parts and limbs in these," he said. "I'll take them back to Nashville with the bodies."

From the other side of the tracks, a man rushed onto the scene. "I heard about the wreck and hurried out here," he said to the undertaker. "My groundskeeper was on the outbound train—it's his day off—he left early to go home to see his family in Kingston Springs along with his brother and cousin."

The man looked through the pile of dead bodies. The undertaker stood next to him. "There he is!" the man cried. "That's Ernest Beck, and there's his brother Oliver lying next to him, and I swear that one lying beneath them is their cousin Jeb." The man looked down the tracks toward the west. Waving his hand in that direction he shook his head, "Their family sure is going to be torn up over this," he said. "No family should bear this kind of grief."

Monsignor Murphy stood up. He'd seen too much suffering and loss; he needed to escape the carnage. He prayed out loud for the departed souls, and sadly walked away.

This photograph and those on the following two pages are courtesy of: The Nashville Public Library, Special Collections.

On a hill above the railroad tracks, the stone cross of Saint Mary's Orphanage beckoned. Monsignor Murphy wearily walked up the hill. Once he got to the orphanage, he found dozens of other passengers waiting there.

No white women or white children were seriously injured in the crash. They were all riding in safety at the back of each train. Now, they mingled on the grounds of the orphanage with the colored women and children who had escaped from the Jim Crow cars without harm.

Many of the white women had been traveling in the ladies' sleeper car on the incoming train. One girl from the sleeper ran toward Monsignor Murphy. "Father! Were you hurt in the crash? I was washing my face when the train stopped. My washbowl flew out of my hands; it shattered in the air. I fell out of my bunk, but I wasn't hurt."

Driveway leading to Saint Mary's Orphanage, Courtesy Metro Archives

A produce truck came up the driveway. The wooden rails surrounding its empty bed rattled and shook as the driver slowed the truck to a stop. He jumped out and rushed to find Sister Mary. "I'm here to carry a load of women and children to Nashville," he said.

Monsignor Murphy and the girl from the sleeper joined Sister Mary and the produce deliveryman. "I'll gladly take that ride," the girl announced. She followed the deliveryman as he headed back to his truck. He was about halfway there when he spun back around.

"I almost forgot, Sister," he called out. "I have a message for you. The garments that were hanging on the corn this morning belonged to the sisters who teach in Memphis. They left on the overnighter Sunday night, but their trunks got misplaced and didn't get shipped until Monday night. The sisters are safe at the Motherhouse. It was only their trunks that were on the train that crashed." He turned and hurried back to his truck.

༄

The sun was setting, and the wrecker derrick stood near the end of Dutchman's Curve. It hovered over the spot where the two locomotives had slammed together about twelve hours earlier. The derrick operator had worked ceaselessly through the day as each damaged car had been removed one by one from the tracks. Now, all that was left to be hauled away from the crash site were the two wrecked locomotives and the boilers that had ripped away from their frames.

Darkness was falling. The task of moving the two giant locomotives would have to wait until morning, but there was still enough daylight to tackle the job of removing the two boilers. DuPont company police and Nashville police officers surrounded the hulking remains of the two wrecked locomotives.

Railroad president John Howe Peyton stood nearby. Even though the locomotives were demolished, they were still valuable, and armed guards were on hand to protect them from vandals and souvenir seekers.

The derrick was positioned near the boiler of Locomotive #281. When the boiler plummeted down in the crash, it landed on the front corner of a Jim Crow car from the Number One train. Now, the wrecker derrick stood next to the spot where the boiler landed, and a crew stood by to attach it to the derrick.

The boiler was attached to the hooks hanging off the derrick boom. The operator lifted the boom and placed the boiler onto a flatcar that rode between the derrick and the steam locomotive. With the boiler secured on the flatcar, the locomotive pulled both the flatcar and the wrecker away from the site.

The locomotive steamed out of view. One of the railroad workers bent down to pick up the debris that was left behind when the boiler was lifted.

"There's people down here!" he shouted. "They're burnt real bad." He looked away from the ghastly sight. "There's a mother holding a child."

Backing away from the scene, he sat down on the ground. "I thought we were through finding dead bodies here." He lowered his head. "I just can't do this anymore."

Wrapping his arms around his legs, he buried his face on his knees. "Somebody else is going to have to move them bodies." he whispered.

Chapter Nine

Dr. Duncan Eve, Jr., walked across the bridge. It was almost dark, and he hurried to reach the car that was waiting on the other side of the bridge to carry him back to Nashville.

Dr. Eve was the NC&StL assistant chief surgeon. On this day, he was in charge of overseeing the medical care of everyone hurt in the accident. At the site, the many doctors and nurses who had rushed out to help had treated more than three hundred injuries, but close to a hundred people suffered life-threatening burns and wounds and had been transported to various local hospitals. Dr. Eve was anxious to get into town and check on them.

He had almost reached the other side of the bridge when he heard someone call out.

"Dr. Eve! You're needed back down on the tracks! We found another pile of dead bodies buried beneath a boiler. We need you to confirm they are dead so we can move them."

The doctor followed the man back down to the spot where the boiler had landed. The six men and three women were burned beyond recognition. The charred remains of the child provided the hardest view.

Nothing angered Dr. Eve as much as having to treat an injury caused by human error. The scene he witnessed filled him with rage. This train wreck was the result of a catastrophic mistake. There was no doubt it had happened because somebody blundered. It was impossible to fathom why an experienced and careful engineer like David Kennedy took his train out onto a single line of tracks *knowing* that another train was on the same set of tracks coming toward him.

Dr. Duncan Eve. Jr. with his daughter Genevieve in 1917.
Courtesy Tennessee State Library and Archives

Dr. Eve had been acquainted with David Kennedy for several years. Not too long ago, the doctor had given the engineer his annual physical examination and even though Kennedy was an aged man in his late seventies, the doctor knew him to be sound of mind and physically fit.

The engineer did have trouble with his vision, and there was already speculation among people who knew him that his poor vision may have contributed to the accident.

As Dr. Eve walked back to the bridge, he thought about the events of the terrible day. In the past, he had been called out to other deadly wreck sites, but this one was the worst scene he'd ever witnessed.

This wreck was even worse than the Circus Train wreck that had happened up in Hammond, Indiana, eighteen days prior. It had been called "the deadliest train wreck in the history of American railroads." Newspapers reported that at least eighty people had burned to death in that collision and that the engineer blamed for causing the wreck had been arrested and charged with their murder.

Now, as Dr. Eve hurried to reach the other side of the bridge, he thought about the changes that needed to be made to improve railroad safety and ensure another calamity like this one never happened again.

৵

Back in Nashville, inside a house in the segregated part of town, a man sat down at his desk. Choosing a *nom de plume*, he borrowed the name of a famous magician. He typed.

The Horrors of the Wreck: A Close Up,

viewed by Prince Mysteria.

He glanced up at the clock on the wall. It was almost nine, and a southbound passenger train carrying two Pullman sleeper cars was scheduled to arrive in Nashville soon. The sleepers were staffed by porters based out of Chicago, and he needed to be down at Union Station to talk to one of them before the train pulled back out and was on its way.

The Chicago Defender—the most read newspaper for people of color—was also based out of Chicago. The Defender was a forum against racial injustice, and Pullman porters often smuggled copies of it into the South, where it was unsafe to possess the incendiary paper.

The porters also smuggled written accounts of racial injustice out of the South. It sometimes took as long as two weeks for them to get back to Chicago and turn in those reports to the newspaper office.

The awful events of this day needed to be reported, and the man intended to send his firsthand account back to the Defender with the first Pullman porters to arrive.

He set his hands back down on the keyboard. He had taken notes throughout the day, and a raging diatribe formed in his mind.

Death walked hand and hand with the passengers of and crews of Trains Number One and Four on Tuesday morning, July ninth, near Nashville, Tennessee, proving that while in life, we are in death.

He looked up at the clock. He typed faster.

In all my experience, I have never been eyewitness to such wholesale murder.

Images of the day whirled through his mind. *Men and women who had left behind loved ones trusting that they would meet again soon, cold and silent, bruised and torn, snatched from life without warning, transported beyond this vale of tears in a twinkling of an eye.*

He recalled one of the saddest stories of the day; two brothers and their cousin perished together. *Two brothers lying side by side on a slab.*

He called to mind all the farmers and laborers who had answered their country's call to duty. *Husbands and wives, fathers and mothers, old and young all coming into a new field, a field of adventure, coming to Nashville to work in the newly constructed powder plant.*

The clock on the wall struck nine. *Coaches constructed of wood, the baggage coach, the Jim Crow section and smoking compartment crowded beyond their capacity. Who will be to blame? Will this serve to remove the Jim Crow section from behind the engine? Also, will it serve to provide the necessary space to prevent overcrowding which is always the case in the Jim Crow car?*

The man stopped typing. He bent his head and rested it on his hands. As long as racist laws forced men and women of color to ride in the most dangerous spot on the train, their lives would be in jeopardy every time they set foot on a railroad boarding platform. Until they gained full equality, any journey they embarked upon would be an unpleasant and perilous odyssey. He put his hands back down on the typewriter, striking hard on the keys. *How long will it take? This is the question and the echo from the cry. How long should echo from the twelve million Negroes throughout the country.*

He pulled the typed sheet out of the typewriter. Slipping his story into a long brown envelope, he hid it inside the breast pocket of his vest. He grabbed his bowler hat off the stand in the corner, slapped it on his head, and rushed out the door.

Chapter Ten

Shortly after nine on this Tuesday evening, Dr. Eve walked through the thirteenth ward of Nashville City Hospital. The hospital was a flurry of activity. Doctors and nurses rushed about. They worked with urgency to make sure that every one of their patients was cared for and that any suffering was relieved as much as circumstances allowed. Taxed to its utmost in caring for the injured, almost every available cot and bed in the hospital was pressed into service. The thirteenth ward was filled to capacity.

As Dr. Eve walked through the ward, he was accompanied by an orderly. Making their way through the turmoil, they stopped at a cot where the body of a young man lay still and fully covered with a sheet. The doctor pulled it down so he could examine the remains.

The dead man's skin was blistered and burned. Dr. Eve reached down and touched the body. He turned and spoke to the orderly. "It took this poor soul a long time to die." The doctor looked away from the burnt corpse, then looked back. "Death came as a relief." He sighed. "What was his name?"

The orderly ran his finger down the list. "His name was Matt Toles. He was one of the powder-plant workers."

Dr. Eve touched the chest of Matt Toles, fingering the sharp shards of broken bones inside the man's crushed rib cage. He said, "Record that this man died of burns and internal injuries."

The orderly jotted down the words as Dr. Eve pulled the sheet back up over the lifeless body. The orderly then dutifully followed the doctor on to the next cot, where another shrouded body lay.

ॐ

Across town in the train shed at Union Station, at about the same time, two men met in secrecy. Protected by the cloak of darkness, they quietly convened on the tracks between two Pullman sleeper cars. One man was a Pullman porter; the other an ordinary Nashville citizen. A plain brown envelope changed hands.

"This is urgent. This is a report of the horror I witnessed out at the train wreck today." The citizen spoke softly and looked over his shoulder anxiously to make sure no one was listening. "It was nothing short of murder!" he hissed. "Hand this over to the editor of *The Chicago Defender* as soon as you get there."

"I don't get back to Chicago for eleven more days," the porter whispered.

"I understand," the man answered. "I would like for my report to get there sooner, but I don't dare send it over the telegraph." He looked the porter squarely in the eyes. "Just promise me that delivery as soon as you return to Chicago."

"I will deliver it first thing. I promise." Reaching out to shake the man's hand, the porter asked, "Who are you?" The porter watched for any human movement around the train, worried someone could have noticed his absence from the sleeper. "When I turn this in, the editor is going to want to know who it came from. Who should I say wrote this?"

The man quietly answered, "Tell him Prince Mysteria wrote it." He doffed his hat.

Bowing in appreciation, he put his hat back on his head, stepped away from the tracks, and quietly disappeared into the night.

Chapter Eleven

At ten o'clock, a lonely train whistle wailed as the overnight train to Hickman, Kentucky, departed Nashville's Union Station. The bloodied tracks at Dutchman's Curve had been cleared of debris, and the westbound train cautiously rolled away from Nashville and on toward the site of the wreck.

Inside the train, the conductor hurried through one of the coaches, collecting passenger tickets. The twenty-five military recruits who had been denied passage earlier in the day filled the back rows. They handed their tickets over to the conductor in silence.

Like thousands of others, the twenty-five young men had rushed to the scene soon as word of the crash reached them. They had witnessed firsthand the fate of their fellow recruits, and now they were approaching the same spot where four of them had died.

The train moved through The Shops. As it passed by the semaphore tower, the train engineer sounded a blast from inside the locomotive. Reaching the place where the double tracks merged into a single line, the train then moved away from The Shops and on toward Dutchman's Curve.

Outside, the crescent moon waxed in the Nashville sky as fireflies flitted about. Down the tracks, along the banks of Richland Creek, water birds rested. Further down the tracks, watchmen stood guard over the hulking remains of the two crashed locomotives.

The night train cautiously rolled through Dutchman's Curve, passing thorough acres of trampled and bloodied cornfields. Passengers inside the train nervously drew back the curtains of the railroad car windows and looked outside as it passed by the demolished locomotives. The train followed the path of Richland Creek as it moved through the curve. Coming out of Dutchman's Curve, the train rolled under the bridge. Up in the cab of the locomotive, the engineer pulled hard on the steam-whistle cord. A long, mournful cry echoed out into the dark as the train moved away from the place where so many had died. Picking up speed, the train raced past Harding Station and into the night. It thundered up hills and raced down through valleys. It sped past farmhouses and made whistle stops in little rural towns. Wailing through the night, the train steamed on toward its destination.

All along the route, the night air was filled with the whistling cry of a Kentucky-bound train.

Part Two

PLACING BLAME

*"The Railroad Administration announced tonight that George
L. Loyall, assistant to the regional director for the South, has
been ordered to Nashville to investigate the wreck on the
N. C. & St. L. Railway. Mr. Loyall is especially charged, the
administration said, with fixing individual responsibility for
the wreck, if that be possible."*

The Nashville Banner
July 10, 1918

Chapter Twelve

On the morning of October 21, 1920, Mary Kennedy, widow of David Kennedy, arrived at the Nashville Public Square with her daughters, Katie Belle and Anna Mae. Clutching her daughters' arms, she walked toward the Davidson County Courthouse. The temperature outside was warmer than usual for this time of year, and pedestrians bustled about the square.

Davidson County Courthouse, 1920, Courtesy Tennessee State Library and Archives

Mary Kennedy was the plaintiff in a lawsuit against both the NC&StL Railway and against James C. Davis, the government agent in charge of running the railroad the day her husband was killed. She walked slowly, her mind occupied with memories of her beloved husband.

She was on a quest to clear his name.

It rattled her convictions to know that many of the people hurrying past—like most of the population of Nashville—blamed him for causing the train wreck out at Dutchman's Curve and held his name in contempt.

She stood still on the sidewalk outside the courthouse doors. Paralyzed by the fear of facing the public contempt inside the courtroom, she looked to her daughters for guidance.

Recognizing their mother's state of mind, her daughters urged her forward. Linking their elbows with hers, they firmly led her up the steps and through the oaken door.

Up on the second story of the courthouse, Mary Kennedy and her daughters stepped into the courtroom. Her attorney, William Norvell, met them there.

William Norvell was a prominent young lawyer. He was a past president of both the Tennessee Bar Association and the Nashville Bar and Library. A leader in Tennessee's march toward progress he was known as a modern trailblazer throughout the South. On this day, he was confident that Mary Kennedy had a strong case and he tried to reassure her and her two daughters as he led them to their seats.

Fidgeting with the stiff collar of her mourning dress, Mary Kennedy sat next to him, silently praying a Novena to Saint Jude, the patron saint of difficult cases. Next to her, William Norvell scribbled down notes as he looked through the stack of papers balanced on his lap.

William Norvell, From the book, *Tennessee's Most Prominent Men*, 1920

Oblivious to the chatter of the spectators behind her, she looked ahead. With her eyes fixed on the chamber door, she watched, waiting for the judge to emerge. The judge in this case was Albert Bramlett Neil. He was a direct and well-reasoned man and she was hopeful that he would give her case a fair hearing.

A deaf woman, Mary was unaware of the hush that fell over the room when the judge finally appeared. The bailiff hollered, "Arise!" and Mr. Norvell signaled her to stand.

The judge pounded his gavel.

The bailiff took his place at the front of the room and called the court to order. "In the Second Circuit Court of Davidson County Tennessee, Mrs. Mary Kennedy, Administratrix, versus the Nashville Chattanooga and Saint Louis Railway, *et al*. The Honorable Albert Neil presiding."

All eyes in the courtroom turned toward Mary Kennedy. It was the Gilded Age of Railroads, and she appeared an unlikely candidate to stand up against such a formidable foe. She was an ailing widow. Born twelve years after the first steam locomotive arrived in Nashville, she had lived in the railroad's powerful shadow her entire life. It was the extreme circumstances of her husband's death that gave her the courage to stand up against it.

At the age of twenty-six, she had married NC&StL Railroad Engineer David Kennedy, enmeshing her life with the railway for the next thirty years. David Kennedy was a popular man with an important railroad job, and her status in the community was a reflection of his good standing. That all changed in the hours following the crash. The train wreck at Dutchman's Curve was the deadliest train wreck in the history of American railroads, and her husband was blamed for causing it right from the very beginning. He was dubbed "The Blunderer" before his body was even removed from the rubble. One-time associates and strangers alike referred to him by that name from that point on. Only a handful of friends defended his legacy.

David Kennedy had been a member of the Nashville Knights of Columbus since it was founded in 1899. Within hours after the accident happened, many of his brother knights disavowed him. Posting a public notice in the evening paper the night after the wreck, the Knights of Columbus called "a special meeting to decide how to treat the memory of our former brother David Kennedy."

The esteem he had held in Nashville for over fifty years disappeared before the debris from the wreck was even cleared away from the railroad tracks. Neither his reputation as a cautious and safe engineer nor his standing as a good and decent man made the public believe otherwise.

On July 11th, two days after the wreck occurred, officials from the Interstate Commerce Commission, the United States Federal Railroad Administration, and the Nashville Terminals of the NC&StL Railway announced "a preliminary investigation to fix responsibility for the accident would commence on Saturday, July 13th." But long before the officials began their investigation, the public had already fixed responsibility for the disaster squarely on the shoulders of David Kennedy. Blame for the wreck was placed almost entirely on him, and no one suffered the scorn of it more than his grieving widow.

Now, two years later, she was suing the NC&StL Railway and Federal Agent James C. Davis to get financial compensation for her husband's death. But more so, she was trying her best to clear his name of responsibility for causing the wreck, and fighting to let his memory rest in peace.

Mary was suing the railroad and Agent Davis under the Federal Employers Liability Act, a law that pertains only to railroad workers. The act compensated railroad workers (or their beneficiaries) for being injured or killed while performing interstate railroad duty. Benefits weren't automatically paid, though. First it had to be proven that the railroad company or one or more of its employees was at least partially responsible for causing the injury or death.

One reason Mary instituted this case was to prove once and for all that David was not responsible for causing the train wreck that claimed his life and killed all those other people. The other reason was to gain financial benefits for herself, her two unmarried daughters, and her son.

Attorney Seth Walker represented the NC&StL Railway in the case brought by Mary Kennedy. Only twenty-seven years old, Walker was a talented lawyer well-versed in previous judgments based on the right of action of the

Federal Employee Liability Act, and was handpicked by the railroad company to handle the proceeding. He was a member of the State House of Representatives. As Speaker of the House in the General Assemblies Extra-ordinary session two months prior, opposed to giving women the right to vote, he had vigorously fought ratification of the 19th amendment. Now, his clients expected him to use that same vigor in this courtroom, in their defense against the disabled widow, Mary Kennedy.

Walker faced the judge. The voice of plaintiff lawyer William Norvell rang out from across the courtroom. "May it please the court, my client Mary Kennedy is stone deaf, Your Honor, and I want one of the daughters to act as interpreter, you might say, on account of her disability."

Judge Neil turned to the defense. "Do you agree?"

"Yes, sir, we have agreed on this," said Walker.

Norvell looked down at his notes. "May it please the court, in order to save time in the examination of this witness, we have agreed that it may be stipulated that Katie Belle Kennedy may testify on just a few facts that I will have to prove by Mary Kennedy. They are as follows: that she is the widow of David Kennedy. That she is qualified as the administratrix of his estate. That she and the deceased were the mother and father, respectively, of the other three beneficiary plaintiffs named in the declaration."

Taking a breath, he read on. "That her husband at the time of his death was in the employ of the Nashville Chattanooga and Saint Louis Railway. That the other defendant was operating same railway at that time. That the deceased had been working for this railway for approximately forty-seven years, and as engineer for some years. That her husband, at the time of his death, was seventy-two years of age and that he was hale and hearty for that age."

Norvell continued his litany of facts. "That at the time of his death, she was fifty-six years of age, now being fifty-eight, and that the condition of her health since the time of the accident has been that she was nervously depressed and rundown, but her general health is fair and that there are no vital troubles that she knows of."

The judge looked back at Walker. "You agree to this?"

"Yes, sir. It is agreed that the daughter would testify to that for her mother," he replied.

Norvell cleared his throat and spoke up. "May it please the court furthermore, sir, it is also agreed that this witness would testify that up to the time of the accident, the deceased provided for herself and family, and was up to that time the sole support of herself and the two young ladies named as beneficiary plaintiffs and their young brother."

The lawyer walked back to his seat and picked up another stack of papers. He handed them up to the judge. "This is the sworn testimony of Miss Katie Belle Kennedy, Your Honor."

Judge Neil addressed the twelve men seated across the room. "These statements made by counsel and sworn to by Miss Kennedy, gentlemen of the jury, will be considered as a part of the record and as evidence of Mrs. Kennedy as if she had been able to testify."

Chapter Thirteen

The bailiff stepped up to the front of the courtroom and called the first witness. "Katie Belle Kennedy!"

Sworn in, she took her seat in the witness stand. She folded her hands in her lap and sat up straight as her mother's lawyer asked her to state her name. She felt the gaze of the jury looking her way, and her voice wavered timidly when she spoke.

"My name is Katie Belle Kennedy." she replied.

Norvell continued, "Miss Katie Belle, how old was your father when this wreck happened?"

With the question directed toward her father and not at her, she felt less bashful and answered with a steadier voice. "Seventy-two," she said.

"Who all was living in your home at that time?"

"My mother, myself, and my sister Anna Mae. And Father, of course."

"How old were you at the time of the wreck?"

"I was twenty-one, sir."

"How old was your sister?"

She looked across the room at her sister Anna Mae. "Twenty-three."

Norvell moved away from the witness stand, giving the jury a better view of Mary Kennedy. Your mother had no occupation except such as is done in the household there?"

"No, sir," she answered again, this time looking over at her mother.

"How old was your brother John George at the time of the accident?"

"My brother was seventeen."

Norvell moved closer to Katie Belle. "This wreck was on July 9, 1918?

For more than two years, her family had suffered the notoriety and tragedy associated with that date. Katie Bell answered the question with a whisper. "Yes."

"What was John George doing at that time?"

Seth Walker jumped up and interrupted, "We object to that question as immaterial."

William Norvell addressed the judge. "I think that it is material to show who the members of the family were."

Shuffling through some papers on on a nearby table, he found what he was looking for and returned to the front of the courtroom. Holding the papers in the air, he spoke to the judge.

"I have authorities from the Supreme Court of the United States which indicate—"

Walker interrupted again. "Understand, may it please the court, I am not objecting to them showing that the boy was dependent on the father for support, but as to where the boy was or what he was doing. That is all immaterial."

Agreeing with Walker, the judge ruled, "It is admissible for him to only show that he was dependent on the deceased."

In frustration, Norvell argued, "The only way I can show his dependence, Your Honor, is through this line of evidence."

The judge looked down at Katie Belle. She looked agitated sitting in the witness stand. Reversing his previous ruling, he spoke kindly to the young woman. "You may answer that last question."

Katie Bell spoke more loudly. "He was in France. In the army."

Norvell picked back up on his previous line of questioning. "Now, prior to the time he went into the wartime service of the United States Army, had he been working and earning money, or had he been dependent on your father?"

Katie Belle smiled at her mother reassuringly and answered, "No, he wasn't working. He was in school."

Norvell continued, "Now, Miss Kennedy, did your father ever advise you and your sister and John George as to how you should conduct yourselves, or what you should do for your mental, physical, and moral development and welfare?"

She answered honestly. "Father had ideas about how all his children should spend their futures. He intended on sending John George on to college as soon as he returned home from the war in France. Father would have done so, if he hadn't been killed."

"How long after the Armistice did John George return?"

"It was about four months, sir."

"So, if your father had lived to see John George come home from the war, your brother would have returned to school and continued on as a dependent of your father. Is that correct?"

86

Seth Walker shot out of his seat. "I object to that question, Your Honor!"

Keeping his back turned to his opponent, William Norvell spoke. "I respectfully withdraw the question, Your Honor."

William Norvell tried to size up the men of the jury. Mary Kennedy was asking for beneficiary compensation in the amount of twenty-five thousand dollars—more than thrice the average amount paid out to the beneficiaries of the thirty-four other white men killed in the wreck.

David Kennedy was older than all but two of those victims. Due to Kennedy's advanced age, the jury would likely view his future earning capacity as less than most of the other men who had died in the wreck.

To justify his client's request for such a large settlement, Norvell planned to show the jury that the deceased railroad engineer was in good health and enjoyed a long life expectancy, and therefore his dependents had had good reason to believe he would be around to support them for many more years to come. Thanks to one unusual set of circumstances, the lawyer was confident the jury would see things his way.

Ever since railroads were nationalized in 1917 there was a general sense of resentment in Nashville toward the federal government for interfering in private enterprise and taking over the NC&StL Railway. And even though the government had returned control of company back to its owners six months prior to this day, that feeling of resentment remained. The fact that the government was in charge when the wreck occurred and would be held liable if Mary Kennedy won this case was a point in her favor.

Assured by what he saw in the faces of the jury, William Norvell turned his attention back to Katie Belle.

"Miss Kennedy, you have given your father's age. Now, please state about his health and his activity and vigor from a mental and a physical standpoint."

"He never complained, and he was very active. I can only remember one time that he was ill. About two years before the accident."

"Now, was he a very stout or large man? What was his physical build? Was he lean and spare? About what, would you say, were his physical characteristics in that regard?"

"He was not stout. He was rather tall and well-built," she answered.

"What about his ability to walk and handle himself?"

"He walked always to work and to the washhouse," she said with pride. "He was very active. You should imagine a man not much over fifty, instead of his age."

William Norvell took a sip of water and wet his lips before tackling what he knew would be some very difficult questions for the young woman to answer.

"Now, Miss Kennedy. Were you at home when this accident happened?"

"Yes," she replied.

Norvell looked over his shoulder to where Mary Kennedy sat. "Was your mother home?"

Taking a deep breath, Katie Belle answered. "Yes."

"John George was away at war in the army. Your sister—where was she?"

The question took Katie Belle off guard, and she paused before answering. "She was visiting in Washington, D.C."

The lawyer spoke with sympathy, "Did you see your father's body, or any portion of his body after the wreck?"

Clenching her folded hands together, she lowered her eyes. "Yes, sir."

The courtroom was silent as Norvell asked the next question. "About how long after the accident?"

"Well, they brought him home about ten o'clock the night of the accident."

"You were not out at the scene of the wreck?"

"No."

"You were at home when they brought his body there?"

"Yes, sir."

Norvell moved closer to Katie Belle, and in a very soft voice asked, "Did you see enough of his body to recognize him as your father?"

She let out a little cry before responding to the question. "Yes. I saw his head and his shoulders."

"How much of his body was it you saw?"

Recalling a terrible memory, Katie Belle grew flustered and didn't know how to answer. "Beg pardon?"

"How much of his body was recovered and brought home?"

Tears clouded her eyes and she choked out her reply. "I couldn't say, Mr. Norvell, because I just saw…"

"You just saw the upper portion?"

"Yes, sir," she whispered.

"In what condition was the upper portion? Particularly, the head?"

Removing a handkerchief from her skirt pocket, she dabbed her eyes as she answered the awful question. "His head was badly swollen, and there was a scar on his face, on the right side, and also on the left side."

William Norvell drifted away from the witness stand. Facing the courtroom, he spoke loudly. "You young ladies were unmarried at the time of the accident?"

Without looking up, Katie Belle folded the handkerchief into a little square. "Yes."

"And still are unmarried?"

"Yes," she said.

Norvell moved toward the judge's bench. "Now, going back a moment, I want to phrase a question a little differently, if I may." He looked over at Seth Walker for a sign of any objection. Seeing none, he continued.

"At the time John George went away to war, how far had he advanced in school? Do you recall, Miss Kennedy?"

"He was in the ninth grade."

"Through primary school?"

"Yes, he graduated primary school about four years before."

Norvell nodded. "I have no more questions for this witness, Your Honor."

William Norvell returned to his seat next to Mary Kennedy as Seth Walker approached the witness stand. Katie Belle ran her hands down the skirt of her dress, smoothing out a wrinkle as he made his way toward her.

"Miss Kennedy, I understand that your father, at the time of his death, was making from two to two hundred and fifty dollars a month. Is that true?" Walker began.

Gripping her hands together she quietly answered. "Yes."

"Now, in addition to that, I understand that he drew a pension."

She responded, "He did."

"From whom did he draw the pension?"

"From the government of the United States. He was in the Civil War."

The lawyer acted surprised. "From the United States government?" he looked at around the room, making eye contact with some of the spectators seated in courtroom. "He was a Union soldier, then?"

Blushing, Katie Belle looked down as she answered. "Yes."

"Now, how much pension did he draw from the United States government?"

Katie Belle lifted her head back up and replied, "He drew seventy-five dollars a quarter, twenty-five dollars a month."

"Now your mother still draws that?"

"Yes she does."

"Do you know why your father drew a pension from the government? Was he disabled?"

"All the old soldiers do. He wasn't disabled."

"Not in any respect?"

"No!"

"Your father was seventy-two years of age, I believe?"

Katie Belle unclenched her hands. Clenching them back together, she answered the question. "Yes."

"You spoke about your father walking to the washhouse. How far was the washhouse from your home in the Aberdeen Railroad Apartments?"

"Well, the washhouse was on Twelfth Avenue, and we lived at Nineteenth and Hayes."

"Well, so, it was four or five blocks he walked?"

"Further than that, sir. More like seven, and then you have to go down several blocks to get there."

"And he walked to Union Station each morning?"

"Yes, sir."

"Did your father ever complain about his back giving out when he came in?"

Katie Belle looked straight into Mr. Walker's eyes. "No," she said.

"What was the condition of his teeth, if you remember— good teeth?"

"My father had very good teeth."

"And he was in good health for a man of his age?"

Trying to conceal her aggravation at Walker's repetitive questions, Katie Belle drew a deep breath before answering. "His health was very good."

"I have one more question for you, Miss Kennedy." Seth Walker said. "Do you know at what age his father died?"

The question embarrassed Katie Belle. Her father had been estranged from his family down in Alabama ever since he ran off and joined Company B of the 38th Ohio Regiment in 1862, and not even her mother had ever met one of his relatives. Katie Belle didn't know a thing about any of them—let alone how old her grandfather had been when he died.

Concealing her embarrassment, Katie Belle calmly answered. "No, I do not."

Chapter Fourteen

Katie Belle held her mother's hand as Malachi Bryan, sharing legal duties with William Norvell on behalf of Mary Kennedy, went forward to begin the direct examination of Anna Mae. A one-time state senator, Mr. Bryan was seventy-one years of age. He was a member of the Nashville Knights of Columbus and had been acquainted with David Kennedy for many years. Unlike so many of his brother knights, Bryan hadn't disavowed the engineer on the occasion of his death.

Bryan cautiously approached Anna Mae. She was nervous. She didn't want to be on the witness stand or answer questions under oath, and Mr. Bryan had promised he would be gentle with his questions and try not to keep her there long.

"Miss Kennedy, what is your first name?"

"Anna Mae."

"Miss Anna Mae Kennedy, you are the daughter of Mrs. Kennedy, that is, the plaintiff in this case?"

Anna Mae nodded her head. "Yes, sir."

"And the late D.C. Kennedy who was killed in the railroad accident which has been described here?"

She nodded her head again. "Yes," she said.

"Had you or sister prior to the time of the death of your father at any time been in any employment?"

This was the question Anna Mae had dreaded answering. In 1917, she had worked as a clerk at a department store downtown, and even though she lived with her parents at that time, she hadn't been completely dependent on her father for financial support because she had taken a job.

She couldn't recall whether it was one of her siblings or the lawyers who first came up with the idea that she should lie about working to make her appear to be more helpless than she was, but she wished she hadn't agreed to take part in the deception. Her heart raced as she uttered the lie. "No."

"Who took care of you?"

"My father."

"He was in railroad service?"

"Yes, sir."

"In what capacity?" the lawyer asked.

"Engineer."

"With what company?"

The men sitting on the defense side of the room represented the company her father had worked for. As far back as she could remember, Anna Mae had been trained to treat railroad company officials with respect and loyalty. The action her mother was taking against the men frightened her, and she was intimidated by their presence.

Aware that railroad company bosses were listening to her every word, Anna Mae concentrated her attention on Bryan.

"He worked for the NC&StL Railway, sir."

"State to the jury how long he had been there, from your knowledge."

Anna Mae faced the jury. "For as long as I can remember."

"He was in the service of the railroad company commencing with your earliest recollection?"

"Yes, sir."

"And with the same company?"

"Yes, sir."

"And in the same capacity as an engineer?"

"Yes, sir."

"Was he an engineer of a passenger train?"

Anna Mae quietly answered the question. "Yes, sir, and as I remember, on the same run."

"State, Miss Kennedy, if you please, whether your father was a home man, stayed much at home?"

"He stayed most of his time at home, when he was off the road."

"What were his relations with your mother and you children, were they intimate and friendly, or otherwise?"

Anna Mae confronted the stares of the spectators in the courtroom. "He was a very kind husband to mother and a loving father to all of us children. He was very considerate and wanted us to have everything we wanted. He looked out carefully for all our needs."

Weary of questions, Anna Mae spoke her mind. "He was a very good father."

As much as it distressed her, Anna Mae's questioning was not over yet.

Bryan continued, "What did he do with his wages when he received them?"

"He turned them over to Mother."

"Please state, Miss Kennedy, whether or not your mother had charge of the expenditures of the funds for the living, support, and dress of the children of the family."

95

Anna Mae's eyes darted across the room. Meeting the gaze of her mother, she answered clearly. "She did."

Mary Kennedy looked unhappy. Unable to hear what was being said, she didn't understand what was happening in the courtroom, and was visibly agitated. Anna Mae tried to maintain her composure on the witness stand to keep from upsetting her more. Breaking away from the gaze of her mother, she turned her attention back to Bryan.

"Did your father maintain any of his wages or moneys for his own expenditures?"

"He retained a small amount for his own personal expenses. I should say forty dollars," she replied.

"Forty dollars a month?"

"Yes," she answered. "Forty dollars a month."

"State to the jury whether or not he took an active interest in his children and their welfare."

Anna Mae spoke to the jury. "He was always interested in everything we did and wanted us to have just as much as anybody else."

"State whether or not he was in the habit of counseling and advising and directing his children?"

Uncomfortable facing the scrutiny of the jury, her face turned red as she responded to his question. "Yes, he was," she answered.

"State whether or not in their development he watched after his children or advised them."

"He did," she said.

"Do you know whether or not he intended that John George should be educated in college?"

"He did."

"Please tell the jury the character and build of man, was your father a large, heavy man or was he a man of medium size and build? Describe to the jury just what kind of build he had."

Anna Mae cleared her throat. "He was rather tall," she said. Turning back to the lawyer, she continued, "A man of about your height, Mr. Bryan, not heavy, he was well built, very muscular."

"Was he physically active?"

"Very." Anna Mae emphatically nodded her head. "He never took the streetcar. He walked everywhere around town."

"Was he energetic or sluggish in his movements?"

"He was very energetic, and I seen him just a few days before I left for Washington, indulged in a very active ball game."

"A what?" the lawyer asked.

"Ball game."

"Baseball?"

"Yes, sir."

"With whom?"

Recalling a happy memory, Anna Mae was at ease as she answered the question. "With some boys from across the street from our house."

Northern soldiers had introduced the game of baseball to the South. Like so many other men who had fought in the Civil War, David Kennedy had learned the game during his term of service, and he enjoyed both playing and watching the game as did most of the men in the jury and many of the spectators in the courtroom.

"How long before his death was that?" Bryan asked.

"That would be about three weeks."

Bryan paused. He stopped talking while onlookers in the courtroom conjured the image of an athletic David Kennedy playing baseball just a few days before his death.

"Now, Miss Kennedy, in regard to the expenditure of money for the support of yourself and your sister and brother, do you know what it cost? And your mother, do you know what the expenditures per month, say, for your mother had been?"

"You mean her personal expenses?"

"Yes, personal expenses."

"Well, I couldn't say just about how much it would be monthly, but I suppose for her clothes and personal expenses not over two hundred dollars a year. Somewhere around that."

"Two hundred a year?"

"Yes, sir. For Mother."

"And what would it be for you and your sister?"

"Our allowance was about seventy-five dollars a month between us."

Walking across the room to where Norvell was sitting, Bryan bent down and asked for a document he was holding. It was a copy of Mary Kennedy's past household budget. Looking the paper over, he handed it back to Norvell and returned to the witness stand.

"Do you know what the running expenses of the house were? Groceries and other things?"

"Well, I can't give you an estimate of each article, but the apartment was forty-seven dollars and fifty cents, the grocery bill was about forty dollars, and the servant, the girl we had we paid a dollar each Saturday, I know that was pretty close to the amount."

"Well, how about the cost of supplies, like table linen, tableware, and things that are consumed in everyday living?"

"Well, I don't know, Mr. Bryan, just about how much that was. Of course, Mother bought everything for the house, I didn't know how much they amounted to."

"Miss Kennedy, you have given us an estimate of the cost of the clothing and personal expenses of yourself, your sister, your father, and mother; state whether or not the remainder of the moneys he collected went toward the household expenses?"

"It did."

"Please state whether or not since your father's death you have gotten employment anywhere?"

"Yes."

"Why did you do that?"

"Because it was necessary to pay the expenses of the house."

"Are you now employed?"

"Yes, sir."

"In what capacity?"

"Music teacher."

"Miss Kennedy, is your mother physically defective in any way? In her hearing?"

"Yes. In her hearing. She is stone deaf."

"She is stone deaf; was she at the time of your father's death?"

"Yes."

"Please state to the jury what is her present condition of health?"

Anna Mae addressed the jury. "Well, her present condition of health is very good."

"Was she ill following the death of your father?"

"Yes. She was ill for quite some time."

"But she recovered?"

"Yes."

"She's as well as she ever was?"

"Yes, sir."

"I have no more questions, Your Honor."

Seth Walker, the opposing counsel, stood. "You can excuse the witness, Your Honor. I have no questions for her at this time."

Anna Mae breathed a sigh of relief, thankful her turn had finally ended.

Chapter Fifteen

William Jones took the witness stand. His wife Mary Kennedy Jones was David Kennedy's firstborn child. Her mother had died when she a little girl, and Mary Daugherty Kennedy was her stepmother.

This morning, Mrs. Jones was noticeably missing in the courtroom. When Mr. Jones had arrived at the courthouse alone, he offered no explanation as to why his wife was absent. Now, as he faced the spectators in the courtroom, a ripple of murmurs drifted around the room as they speculated on the cause of her absence.

Bits and pieces of whisperings rose above the din.

"Embarrassed."

"Dislikes her stepmother."

"Ashamed of her father."

"Never got over the shame of the wreck."

William Jones had become accustomed to hearing gossip about his wife and her family ever since the accident happened two years prior, and he tuned out the courtroom whispers as he answered attorney William Norvell's first searching questions.

"You are Mr. William Jones?"

"Yes, sir."

"What is your occupation, Mr. Jones?"

"I am an embalmer with Dorris, Karsh, and Company."

"You are the husband of the daughter of Mr. and Mrs. Kennedy, who is not a party to this suit?"

"Yes, sir."

"Now, Mr. Jones, how long had you known Mr. Kennedy prior to his death?"

"I had known Mr. Kennedy about twenty years."

"How long had your known him intimately? Have you been in his family that long?"

"No, I have been in the family about seventeen years."

"You came into pretty intimate contact with him then. You visited back and forth?"

"Yes, sir."

"Now, Mr. Jones, what build man was your father-in-law?"

"Mr. Kennedy was a man, I suppose, six foot, maybe an inch over, and would weigh about a hundred and eighty-five pounds, I should judge."

"In regard to his physical activity, Mr. Jones? How was he, active?"

"Very active. He was very active."

"Did you ever observe him at home in the presence of his family?"

"I have."

"You and your wife lived in Nashville, and you visited?"

"Oh, yes."

"What were his disposition and actions?"

"His disposition..."

"What was his disposition between his widow and these two young ladies and John George? The members of the family who are suing, was it kindly and affectionate, or not?"

"It certainly was."

"Was he or not a man who neglected either his wife or his children?"

"Not that I ever knew of. I don't think he ever did."

"He was a good family man?"

"He certainly was."

Attorney Norvell took stock of the jury. He changed his course of questions.

"Mr. Jones, do you remember this wreck in which your father-in-law lost his life?"

"I do."

"Where was the wreck?"

"The wreck was out on the railroad tracks right close to Saint Mary's Orphanage, this side of the overhead bridge."

"Did you go out there?"

"I went out there, sir."

"How long were you there after the wreck occurred? About what time did you get there?"

"I was at Union Station the morning he went out. Seen him go into the dispatcher's office. I didn't speak to him that morning. I just went on home for breakfast and the telephone rang. I learned about the wreck then. I knew he was in it, but I didn't say anything to my wife. I just rushed right out there." William Jones spoke clearly as he recalled the events of that dreadful morning. "I was there about twenty or thirty minutes after the wreck occurred. I was there before the wreckers got there."

"Now, Mr. Jones, in general terms, how would you describe the condition out there? Where was your father-in-law's engine? And the other?"

"Now, of course, I don't know the exact positions of the engines, but if I remember right, his engine was on the right side of the track."

"His engine was going out?"

"Yes, sir, the coaches were telescoped, and the boiler of his engine was lying to the right of the track."

"They were all torn to pieces?"

"Yes, sir."

"Did they find his body?"

"Yes."

"Were you there at the time they found it?"

"Yes, sir, I was there about two, two-and-a-half hours when they discovered his body under the engine. A certain party came to me. I went there and told him it was my father-in-law's body. I climbed down in that debris where the body was supposed to be, and lifted a paper off of his face, and recognized it was him." Jones stopped talking. Taking a folded bandanna out of his suit pocket, he coughed into the dark square cloth. Clearing his throat, he continued. "His face was black and dirty, but I knew it was him. He had a prominent nose."

"Where was he?"

"All down under the wheels and iron, debris all over him, he was under the mess."

"Heavy beams, wheels, iron, and wood?"

"Just a mass of wreckage down under there. We could just see his head and shoulders."

"Were you there while it was being taken out?"

"No, sir, I wasn't. I came back to town with a trainload of dead that they had brought out of one of the coaches, and they said it would be an hour or more before they could begin over there and lift the debris off his body. I went back to town with those bodies to dispose of them. When I started back to the wreck, I met a wagon going back into town. The wagon had his body in it."

Jones braced himself for the next question. He was an experienced embalmer. He had prepared hundreds of bodies for burial, but the sight of David Kennedy's remains was almost too gruesome to recall. He didn't look forward to telling a room full of strangers and thrill-seekers what the condition of his father-in-law's body had been after the wreck.

"Mr. Jones, how much of your father-in-law's body was recovered?"

"They only recovered from a little above his hips. Some of his limbs we never did find."

"They were cut in two?"

"Cut in two, evidently, and burned."

Many of the spectators sitting in the courtroom had never heard before that parts of David Kennedy's body been consumed by fire in the wreck. Gasps of horror erupted throughout the room.

Ignoring the reaction of the audience, Norvell asked another gruesome question. "With reference to the body, what would you say the condition of his head was?"

"His head was scalded. His body was scalded."

"Was his head swollen?"

"Swollen? Yes, sir, very badly."

"Was the portion of the body you saw burned?"

"The reason I said the body was burned was that the burn tendered the flesh at the lower abdomen, showing the lower part must have burned away."

With nothing left to say about his father-in-law's body, Jones sadly shook his head and sighed.

William Jones remained in the witness stand as Norvell wandered away. Facing Mary Kennedy, the lawyer nodded at her, signaling that she was going to be the focus of the next questions.

"Now, Mr. Jones, you also came into contact with your mother-in-law, Mrs. Kennedy, did you not, after you were married?"

"I certainly did. Yes, sir."

"Is Mrs. Kennedy stone deaf?"

"Yes, sir, she certainly is."

"Do you know whether or not she had any vital trouble or is in fair health?"

"I don't understand the question, Mr. Norvell."

"I say, do you know whether or not she is in fair health, or if she has any vital troubles?"

"She isn't ill at the present time, no, sir."

"She was sick after this accident?"

"Yes, sir. She was quite ill for some time. "

"Now, Mr. Jones, you saw your father-in-law down at the Union Station that morning?"

"I saw Mr. Kennedy in the station, yes, sir. Seen him go into the dispatcher's office underneath the train master's office there. I was shipping a body on that early morning train."

"I believe you said you didn't speak to him."

"No, sir, I didn't."

"What did his condition appear to be that morning?"

William Jones sucked in a ragged breath before answering. He had been very fond of his father-in-law, and it was still painful to remember that day.

"He seemed about cheerful as usual; he had on his cap and was going into the train dispatcher's office. I was late for breakfast, I didn't go down and talk to him when I seen him there. I generally went down and talked to him when I seen him at the station, but I didn't on that morning. I just went on home to breakfast."

"Do you know about how old Mr. Kennedy was?"

"About. Yes, sir, I do."

"Approximately what was his age?"

"About seventy-three."

"Now, Mr. Jones, what would you say as to his physical activity and vigor, as compared to an average man of his age?

William Jones looked over at the jury. Answering with the right of someone who knew the deceased well, he replied emphatically. "Well, he was more active than any man I ever knew at his age."

William Novell approached the bench. "I have no more questions for this witness, Your Honor."

Defense attorney Seth Walker had remained silent throughout the direct examination of Jones, but now it was time for his cross-examination. Starting at the point where Norvell left off, Walker abruptly presented his opening question.

"You say Mrs. Kennedy is now in good condition?"

"No, sir, I wouldn't consider her in good health now. She doesn't look like the same woman, really, since this trouble has come on her. She has lost weight. She is awful nervous. She is a nervous wreck."

Walker ran his finger down one of the many pages in his hand. Finding what he was looking for, he asked a new question.

"You say you reached the wreck that morning about twenty or thirty minutes after it happened?"

"I guess I was out at the wreck in twenty or thirty minutes. Don't know for sure, but I guess so."

"Do you know what time the wreck happened?"

"It must have happened a few minutes after seven o'clock."

"You drove out there in an automobile?"

"I went out there in an automobile. Yes, I did. When I first got there, there weren't more than seven or eight other auto driving-machines there. Just a few of them. Weren't many there at all."

"Now, when you got out there, you saw that the two trains had collided?"

"Yes, sir."

"He was pulling the train that was known as Number Four, wasn't he?"

"Yes, sir. Going out."

"And the train which his train collided was the inbound train coming into the shed at Nashville, known as the Number One?"

"Yes."

"They were both passenger trains?"

"Yes. They were both passenger trains."

"His train, the one that pulled out of Union Station was a called a flag train, that is to say, that it stopped at every station?"

"I don't know anything about that, sir."

"You don't know about that? Well, the Number One train with which he collided was a fast train, wasn't it?"

"I don't know for sure, but I suppose it was."

"Had sleepers on it?"

"Yes, it did."

"Now, when you got there, you saw both of the locomotives—both the one that your father-in-law was driving and the one with which he had collided. They were turned over and demolished, and practically torn all to pieces, weren't they?"

"They certainly were, sir. Yes."

"And the first three or four cars on the train that he was pulling had become telescoped and were piled up on top of each other?"

"They were telescoped, yes, sir. Yes. At least one was telescoped. I know it was."

"You saw dead people lying everywhere, didn't you?"

"I certainly did. Yes, sir."

"How many people did you take out of that wreck and bury?"

"I have really forgotten the actual number that our firm handled from that wreck."

"As a matter of fact, there were eighty-seven passengers killed and some fourteen railroaders. Does that sound right to you?"

"Something like that. Maybe a few more. Yes, sir. That sounds about right."

"More than two hundred injured, would you say?"

"Yes, sir. That's what I heard."

"I have no more questions, Your Honor."

"You are excused sir," Judge Neil told William Jones. "Court is adjourned for one hour!"

Chapter Sixteen

Proceedings in the trial of Mary Kennedy versus the NC&StL Railway were about to resume for the afternoon, and James Preston "Shorty" Eubank was the next witness. He paced the sidewalk in front of the courthouse.

Life certainly wasn't being fair to him. Although he hadn't paid the ultimate price—like David Kennedy did—for the blunders made on the morning of the train wreck, he had paid dearly.

Soon after the wreck occurred, he was stripped of his position as a passenger train conductor. Friends and acquaintances shunned him. Strangers turned him into an object of ridicule.

A little more than two years had now gone by since the wreck had occurred, and some of the turmoil it caused him was finally beginning to settle down. His friends were starting to warm back up to him, and it had been a while since he noticed any strangers pointing their fingers in his direction.

Getting subpoenaed to court to testify on behalf of Mary Kennedy was a setback. Her lawyers were sure to ask questions he would rather not answer. He was going to have to sit at the front of the crowded courtroom and talk about the actions he took that morning before the train wreck happened.

Court would resume at one. Eubank took out his old railroad watch. It was fifty minutes past twelve. Taking his time, he followed the courtroom crowd as they filed back inside. He was in no hurry. He had no desire to be forced to talk about events that he'd spent almost every waking moment of the past two years trying hard to forget.

Mary Kennedy's primary attorney, William Norvell, stood at the front of courtroom as Eubank took the witness seat. The moment was finally at hand, and the uncomfortable questioning process began.

"Mr. Eubank, where do you live?"

Eubank answered the question with deference to the lawyer's social standing. "I live at 1113 Sigler Street, Captain."

"In Nashville, Tennessee?"

"Yes, sir."

"What is your present occupation?"

"Working in a machine shop."

"For whom?"

"The NC&StL ."

"Out in The Shops? In West Nashville?"

"Yes, sir."

"Mr. Eubank, how long have you been in the employ of the railroad? How long in one capacity or another, approximately?"

"About thirty-seven or thirty-eight years."

"On July 9, 1918, at the time of the train accident, what was your position with the railroad then? What did you do?"

"Conductor."

"You were running on Number Four that morning?"

"Yes, sir."

"After the accident, Mr. Eubank, did the railway displace you as a conductor and put you in the machine shops?"

From a chair on the defense side of the room, Defense Attorney Seth Walker sprang to his feet. He feared that if the jury heard how Eubank had been demoted after the wreck, they might not understand that the demotion was a result of Eubank failing to follow company rules and not because he owned any part of causing the wreck. The sound of Walker's voice resounded throughout the courtroom.

"We object to that!"

Without hesitation, Judge Neil responded. "Objection sustained."

Norvell was prepared for the objection, and he quickly rephrased his question. "How long did you remain a conductor after the accident?"

"As a conductor?" Eubank asked. His nervousness was getting the better of him.

Walker spoke out. "We object!"

The judge ruled. "I will let him answer the question."

Not sure what to do, Eubank looked to the judge. With a slight nod of his head, Judge Neil gave Eubank the go ahead to speak.

"I wasn't conductor any longer than that day. I wasn't conductor after the wreck happened."

"How long had you been a conductor prior to that time?"

"Thirty years."

"On the morning of the accident, Mr. Kennedy was the engineer on the train?"

"Yes, sir."

"Mr. Eubank, how long had you been running with Mr. Kennedy?"

"Oh, something like three years, I reckon. I can't say for sure Captain."

"The two of you mostly worked together, and were familiar with one another's work habits, and knew what to expect of each other?"

"Yes, sir. We did."

William Norvell adjusted his tie. Loosening the neckband, he asked his next question. "Now, Mr. Eubank. Do you recall what time the Number Four train was due to leave Union Station on the morning of the accident?"

"I think it was due to leave at seven o'clock at that time."

"So Number Four was the train you and Kennedy were running?"

"Yes, sir."

"Number Four on its usual run would leave the Union Station at seven o'clock, as you recall, going out west toward the overhead bridge and Harding Station?"

"Yes, sir."

"Where was the terminus to that train? Where would it have stopped finally, where did it run to? I don't mean on that morning of course. I mean regularly, where did it stop at?"

Our schedule went to Hickman, Kentucky; that is the one we run through on."

"And it was to Hickman, Kentucky, that the train was starting out to that morning. That is where it would have ended up if there had been no accident?"

"Yes, sir."

"I believe you said that your leaving time was seven o'clock that morning. Did you all get off on time?"

"We left about seven-o'-five, as well as I remember leaving there."

113

"Did you get any orders that morning?"

"Yes, sir, we received our orders down in the dispatcher's office."

"Well now, who gave you the order?"

"The operator."

"He gave a copy to you? Did he give a copy to Kennedy?"

"Yes, sir. To both of us."

"You saw when he delivered the order to Kennedy?"

"Yes, sir. I did."

"Now, what kind of train was it that you were running on that morning? I mean, was it a fast train or a slow train?"

"Well, I considered it a fast train, but it was called a local train, stopped everywhere nearly."

"That was a passenger train?"

"Yes, Captain. The Number Four was a passenger train. A local."

"The train was, of course, composed of an engine, a tender, and a baggage car?"

"Yes. It also had a combination mail and baggage car."

"Did you all carry a sleeper car?"

"No, sir. Just five big coaches. For passengers to ride in."

William Norvell quickly scanned the courtroom. One of his subpoenaed witnesses had been absent from the room when court reconvened after lunch. He checked to see if his missing witness had showed up yet, before asking the next question.

"Mr. Eubank, do you remember what your orders were that morning?"

"What the orders were, sir?"

"Yes. The orders that you and Mr. Kennedy picked up at the dispatchers office."

114

"Well, I don't remember exact, Captain. I remember, of course, the biggest words of it."

William Norvell addressed the judge. "May it please the court, Your Honor, I have Mr. Templeton from the railroad under subpoena, but he hasn't gotten here. He is bringing a copy of the order. What I want from him is the order."

Waving a paper in the air, Attorney Seth Walker interrupted. "I have the order." Turning the paper over to the bailiff, Walker sat back down.

Norvell took the copy of the order and turned his attention back to the witness. "To refresh your memory, Mr. Eubank, I hand you what purports to be a copy of that order. It was produced by counsel for the railroad. Read it please, and see if you can recollect that it's the order."

Eubank studied the paper. "Yes, sir, this looks like the order we received that morning. The wording of it is familiar."

"May I see the order, Mr. Eubank?" Norvell reached for the paper. "Might I read it here to you? See if I read it correctly."

"Yes, sir, you can read it to me."

"It's headed here, 'Nashville Chattanooga and Saint Louis Railway, Form Nineteen, Order Number Twenty-Nine, Nashville, July 9, 1918, to Conductor and Engineer.'" Norvell looked up at Eubank. "'Number Four, Engine #282, hold main track until Number One, Engine #281 passes. Meet Number Seven Engine #215 at Harding.' Is that correct? That is the order you received that day?"

"Yes, sir. That's the order."

"Mr. Eubank, what was Train Number Seven?"

"Number Seven is what we call an accommodation train. A passenger train."

"What was Number One?"

"Number One was a passenger train."

"Which one was due in Nashville first? The Number One or the Number Seven train?"

"Number One was due in first."

"What time was Number One due? In other words, what was the scheduled time for Number One to arrive?"

"Seven-ten."

"So you were scheduled to leave ten minutes before Number One was scheduled to pull in? Is that right?"

"Yes, sir. That's right."

"Now, when she, Number One, was on time, where would you generally meet her?"

"Sometimes she would pull into the shed before we could pull out."

"That was when you were running a little late?"

"We might be late, or sometimes she would be a little ahead of time. Not often."

But we mostly met between Union Station and The Shops. Somewhere along the double tracks."

"The double tracks? What if she didn't go by before you left the double track? What would you do? Not on the day of the wreck, of course, but in general."

"We would wait there at The Shops until she went by. But we almost always met her going by on the double tracks."

Norvell raised his arm with a dramatic flourish. Brandishing the train orders in the air, he referred to them as he resumed his direct examination of Shorty Eubank.

"Mr. Eubank, when you got your copy of the order, to whom did you show it or give it?"

"I gave it to the flagman, Sinclair, but I read it to George Hall the porter first, and of course, before that, Mr. Kennedy and I read the orders to one another."

"Your porter was a colored man?"

"Yes, sir."

"Was he killed in the wreck, or not?"

"He was killed."

"He had been running with you some time, had he?"

"He had been running with me some time on that run."

"Your flagman, how long had he been running with you on that run?"

"That was his first trip out with me."

"Then, as far as you know, it was his first run on a passenger train?"

Shaking his head no, Eubank repeated his answer. "I said it was his first trip out with me."

"Do you know whether or not he had run on any passenger trains before that?"

"No, sir, I do not know if he had or if he had not."

"Where was the usual position of the porter on the train?"

"Up in the first coach. The head coach."

"Where was the usual position of your flagman while your train was in motion?"

"Well, leaving here, he would catch the rear end and go through and meet me, and I would give him the train order."

"Where did he meet you that morning?"

"When did I give him the order?"

"Yes, sir. What part of the train did you meet him in to give him the train order?"

"I think it was in the ladies' car, second coach."

"How far had the train proceeded?"

"I believe it was just this side of The Shops that I met him."

"Now, Mr. Eubank, rules of the railroad require the conductor on a passenger train to show or give their order to the flagman, and the engineer to show or give a copy of the order to the fireman. Is that correct?"

"I suppose that's the rule."

Seth Walker called out. "I object to that! The rule is the best evidence, Your Honor." Shuffling through a railroad rulebook, he approached the bench.

Judge Neil responded. "I sustain the objection."

Norvell held his hand out to Walker. "Please hand me your rulebook. I'd like to see it." Walker passed the book over. Thumbing through it, Norvell returned to the witness stand. "Mr. Eubank, you men were all furnished a copy of the rulebook. Weren't you supposed to familiarize yourself with it?"

"Each of us has a rulebook."

"You recognize that as the rulebook of the Nashville Chattanooga and Saint Louis Railway?"

"It looks very much like the rulebook."

"I hand you this book, and want you to look at the second sentence of Rule Two Hundred and Eleven A, and see whether I read this correctly. 'On passenger trains, conductors must show all train orders to the flagman, and enginemen must show the fireman." Eubank accepted the book. "I ask you to please state whether or not your rules provided that on passenger trains, the conductors shall show all train orders to the flagman, and enginemen shall show all their orders to the fireman? Isn't it so stated in the book?"

Eubank closed the book. "That is the way it is stated there."

"That is what you did? You complied with the rule that morning?"

"Yes. I gave my orders to the flagman."

"You gave your orders to the flagman expecting he would look out for Number One?"

"Yes, sir. Look out for Number One. That's just what I expected him to do."

Chapter Seventeen

In 1920, most people living in and around Nashville believed that Kennedy was primarily responsible for causing the big train wreck. They also believed that Eubank was remiss in his duties on the morning of the wreck and that his actions played a role in causing the wreck.

In order to win this case, Mr. Norvell would have to convince the twelve men on the jury that the actions of at least one railroad employee *other* than David Kennedy contributed to causing the wreck. It was with that thought in mind that Mary Kennedy's lawyer went after Shorty Eubank on the witness stand.

"Now, Mr. Eubank, as your train proceeded, you were supposed to be looking out for the Number One train. While your train proceeded, pulled out of the station, went through the yards and out through The Shops on in the direction of where the accident occurred, what were you doing?"

Shorty Eubank sighed. Over the past two years, he'd been asked this question more than a dozen times. No matter how he formed the answer, it always ended up making him look bad. "I was taking up tickets to see where the passengers were going to."

"Did any train at any time pass by while you were taking up tickets?"

"There was something passed by my train on the double track out in The Shops. I couldn't say for sure that it was a train that went by. All I know is that it was something with steam."

"So, something with steam passed by. Now did your porter or your flagman at any time before the collision come advise you that something with steam had passed? Did they tell you about a train or anything else?"

"No, sir."

"Did you ask them?"

"I didn't see either one of them after the thing with steam passed until after we hit." Images of that morning filled his mind. He regretfully finished his answer. "George Hall—the porter—he was dead by then."

"About how far is it from the place you saw something with steam pass to where the accident happened?"

"About two miles, I reckon it was."

"It happened at what they call Dutchman's Curve?"

"Yes, sir."

"Out by the Catholic orphan asylum?"

"Yes, sir."

"After you passed this train, or this thing with steam in it, your train went on its regular course on by The Shops, by the tower, and on out on to the single track. There is a single track past the tower?"

"Yes, sir. It's single track all the way to Harding after you leave The Shops."

Eubank was tired of sitting in the witness stand. He felt like he'd been answering questions all day. As Mr. Norvell asked his next question, the one-time conductor fought the urge to take out his trusty railroad watch to see exactly how long he'd been sitting up there on display.

"In going through the yards at that time of morning, are there usually some switch engines passing around?"

"Yes, there are usually switch engines between Nashville and The Shops, scattered about in different places."

"When the thing with steam went by, where were you in your train? Did you go to get a look out at what was passing?"

"I tried to look out the window, but the car was full of standing people. I couldn't get out to see, and then I went back to taking up tickets. Like I said, I couldn't see what it was, people, they blocked the aisle so I couldn't get around, couldn't get out to see."

"Was this engine, train, or whatever it was, was it on the track that Number One was supposed to pull in on, or not?"

"Yes, sir."

"When your train went out on past the tower and The Shops, and got on that main track, did you know whether Number One had passed you or not?"

"No, sir. I did not."

"You did not stop the train or give any signal to the engineer to stop?"

"No, sir."

"Now, just exactly what control, I mean in regard to physical equipment, does a conductor have over a train? In other words, if he should want to stop a train, or should think it should be stopped, can he pull the bell cord to notify the engineer?"

"Yes, sir. And if the engineer don't stop, the conductor can pull another cord."

"The angle cock?"

"Yes. The emergency valve."

"In other words, the conductor can stop the train by signaling the engineer, or by working the emergency valve himself?"

"I reckon working the emergency valve would stop the train."

"Now, in regard to the first means of communication I asked you about. You do have a signal, don't you, that is understood on your road—by a simple pull of the bell cord, that indicates the conductor wants the train stopped?"

"Yes, sir."

"How many times do you pull?"

"Pull twice while he is running."

"That was thoroughly understood by engineer and conductors on your road? That while running, two pulls on the bell cord was the signal that the conductor wanted the train stopped? That the conductor wanted the engineer to stop the train?"

"Yes, Captain. It was understood."

Mr. Norvell moved away from the witness stand. He picked up a photograph from the nearby table. Holding the photograph up high, he showed it to Mr. Eubank.

"Do you know where this concrete bridge is? Over the tracks out by, Saint Mary's, the orphan asylum?"

"Yes, sir."

"With reference to this bridge, where did the collision take place?"

"Right on this side of it."

"It was a head-on collision, wasn't it?"

"Yes, sir."

"A pretty bad wreck, the engines were broken all up, some of the cars telescoped, and a great many people killed and injured, that is correct, isn't it?"

Eubank gripped the arms of his chair and answered. "Yes, sir."

"Now, of your train crew, how many were killed in that wreck?"

Eubank's knuckles turned white. "Three of them."

"Mr. Kennedy was killed. Was his fireman killed?"

"His name was Luther Meadows. That was his fireman."

"Was he killed?"

"Yes, sir."

"And you said the porter was killed?"

"Yes, sir. He was."

"Did you ever see the flagman after the accident?"

"No, sir, not on that day."

"Have you seen him at all?"

"I seen him one day a few days after the wreck."

"Do you know where he lives now?"

"No, sir, I don't. Didn't know where he lived then and don't know where he lives now."

The whereabouts of the flagman Sinclair was a mystery. Four days after the wreck, he'd showed up at the railroad office for the investigation interrogation, but he left town soon after that. No one in Nashville had come forward to say that they had seen or heard from him since he'd disappeared.

Eubank honestly didn't know anything about the missing flagman, and he was relieved when Norvell changed the subject.

"When you were with Mr. Kennedy that morning at Union Station when the order was given, did he appear to be in his usual good health?"

"Yes, sir. I didn't see any change in him. At least, I didn't notice any."

"After you picked up your orders, did you see him anymore?"

"We walked from the telegraph office over to the train together, one or two tracks over. But I never did see him alive after that. "

"Did you ever see his body after the wreck? Did you see him taken out?"

"I seen his body up at the undertaker's shop."

"You never saw the location of his body out at the wreck?"

"No, sir."

Norvell edged closer to the witness stand. "Mr. Eubank." he said quietly. "When that engine or train or whatever-it-was passed you out there, I am asking you whether or not you didn't think it was Number One? Is that the reason you didn't stop the train?"

The whole time he'd been in the witness stand, Eubank was aware that Mary Kennedy was watching his every movement. He knew her to be a good woman who had suffered greatly since the wreck. And he hoped the answer he was about to give wouldn't upset her once her daughters communicated his comments to her.

"Well, Kennedy was on the head end where he could see the number of the engine and everything else, and I never gave it any more thought. I just supposed it must have been Number One, since he kept going."

Quickly changing the subject, Norvell came at his witness with a new set of questions. "Now Mr. Eubank, how far on the other side of The Shops does Dutchman's Curve start?"

"I think it's about halfway between the four- and five-mile posts, past Union Station."

"Did you look at your watch when you passed the tower in The Shops?"

"No, sir."

"Well, while you didn't time yourself, or look at your watch when you passed the tower, you do know that from the time the train passed the tower to the time of the collision occurred that several minutes elapsed?"

"Yes, sir."

William Norvell stepped away from the witness stand.

"I have no more questions for this witness at this time, Your Honor."

Railroad defense attorney Seth Walker moseyed up to the witness stand to begin his cross-examination of Shorty Eubank, the former conductor who had been summoned to court by the plaintiff. Eubank was a long-time employee and Walker was confident that under cross-examination he would give answers favorable to the defendants. Few companies in Tennessee commanded the kind of loyalty that the Nashville Chattanooga and Saint Louis Railway received from its workforce and Eubank was known to be faithful.

⁂

Meanwhile, a few blocks away, a committee of NC&StL company officials met in a third-floor office of the railroad's General Office Building. The building functioned as company headquarters. It stood across the street from Nashville's Union Station, and had been a hubbub of activity ever since the government had reverted control of the railroad back to the company in March.

The same day that Seth Walker was busy fighting to prove in court that the company bore no responsibility for the wreck; the officials were hard at work developing a plan to improve safety on the NC&StL Railway line.

In a scathing report penned on August 16, 1918, the chief of the Bureau of Safety, Federal Agent W. P. Borland condemned the railroad for not having a modern signal system in place.

He wrote, "This accident would have been prevented, beyond question of doubt, by a properly operated manual block system on the single-track line north of The Shops, for which all necessary appliances and facilities were already available." Borland also faulted the railroad company for employing the use of wooden passenger cars. "This accident presents a more appalling record of deaths and injuries than any other accident investigated by the Commission since the accident-investigation work was begun in 1912. Had steel cars been used in these trains, the toll of human lives taken in this accident would undoubtedly have been very much less."

With the government in control of the company at the time of the wreck, and with NC&StL officials acting mostly as figureheads, the railroad officials wielded limited clout within the company. They did, however, have the power to hire and fire personnel. They came together with stockholders and government agents to fire company president John Howe Peyton.

Peyton had only been the NC&StL president for four years. He was from Virginia, and was considered an outsider by the tight-knit railroad community. No one contested his termination.

Less than three weeks after Borland's report was made public, the ousted president shot himself in the head. He died in the bedroom of his lavish mansion, just six blocks from his former seat of power at the General Office Building.

Now, two years later, company officials were finally in charge of running the railroad again. Train crew and passenger safety were their primary concerns, and repairing the public image of the NC&StL Railway was high on their agenda.

Although twenty-six NC&StL railroad workers had been killed in train wrecks since 1911, only one *passenger* on the line had died from injuries sustained in a train wreck during that time. The enormity of the 1918 crash was a stain on the company's record.

Among the first orders of business for the officials were installing an improved signal system up and down the line, and replacing wooden coaches on all fast passenger trains with coaches made of steel.

Chapter Eighteen

Back in the courtroom, Attorney Seth Walker had the chance to ask Shorty Eubank a few questions of his own.

"Mr. Eubank. What is your age?"

"My age? I'm fifty-seven."

"How long have you been employed by the NC&StL Railway?"

"I commenced to railroad in '83. About thirty-seven years."

"You started with them here at Nashville, did you?"

"Yes, sir."

"In what capacity?"

"Well, I started in first as a brakeman."

"How long were you a brakeman?"

"Seven years, I believe it was. All told."

"Brakeman on a freight train, not a passenger train?"

"Yes, sir."

"After you ceased to be a brakeman, what did you do?"

"I ran a train."

"A freight train conductor?"

"Yes. A freight conductor."

"And how long were you a freight conductor?"

"I ran a freight train until 1905, I believe it was, before I was promoted to running a passenger train."

"Now Mr. Eubank, let's go back to the morning in question. You were conductor and Mr. Kennedy was engineer on the Number Four train? You and Mr. Kennedy worked together for some time, did you?"

"Yes, sir. I ran the train with Uncle Dave for quite some time." The nickname he'd used for his long-gone crony caught in his throat as he said it.

Ignoring Eubank's emotional reaction Walker asked his next question. "You were conductor, and Mr. Kennedy was the engineer on the train known as the Number Four?"

"Yes, sir."

"You had Meadows as your fireman, a Negro porter, and Sinclair as your flagman.

"Sinclair was injured some in the wreck, was he not?"

"How is that, sir?"

"He was injured to some extent in the wreck, Sinclair was?"

"I can't tell you that. He was down there at the General Office a few days after the wreck. I saw him there. He seemed fine. That was the only time I have seen him other than when I saw him on the train. That was the only two times I ever seen him in my life."

Seth Walker held up a photograph. "This Negro porter, George Hall, was he killed?"

"Yes, sir."

"And Mr. Kennedy the engineer, and Mr. Meadows the fireman—both were killed on Number Four?"

"Yes, sir."

"Train Number Four was a train that stopped at all flag stations?"

"Yes, sir." Eubank paused to reconsider. "Well, it didn't stop at all flag stops unless we had someone getting off there."

"It wasn't what you called a 'through train?'"

"No, sir, it was a local."

"In railroad parlance, it is known as a 'local?'"

"Yes, a local. You see, what we call a flag station may just be a road crossing."

"The Number One train was running from Memphis, Tennessee, to Nashville, Tennessee?"

"Yes, sir."

"The Number One train. It was what was called a 'through train' or a 'fast train?'"

"Not a through train. Not the whole way. Just a through train from Dickson."

"A through train from Dickson?"

"It don't make any stops after there except by special orders."

"In other words, Dickson, Tennessee, —about forty miles distant from Nashville—was the last stop Number One made prior to arriving at Union Station?"

"Yes, sir."

"Now, there is what is known on the railroad as a 'superior train' and an 'inferior train'—is that right?"

"Yes, sir.

"Train Number One was a superior train. Train Number Four was an inferior train. Is that right?"

"Yes, sir."

"Now, being a superior train, Number One had the right-of-way. Is that correct??"

Betraying the memory of his friend, Eubank squirmed under the gaze of Mary Kennedy as he answered the question. "Yes, sir. Number One had rights to the track. Uncle Dave never should've taken Number Four out there without knowing for certain that Number One had passed."

⌇

Shorty Eubank was an active man, and accustomed to working on his feet. Sitting on the witness stand was wearing him out. He wished Walker's cross-examination would hurry up and end.

"Now, that morning, you got down to Union Station sometime before seven o'clock?"

"Always did, sir."

"What track number did Train Number Four pull out on from Union Station?"

"The westbound track on the east side of the station. I believe it is track Number Three."

"That was the track it pulled out on every other morning?"

"Yes, sir."

"What track did Number One come in on every morning?"

"I couldn't tell you, Captain. It comes in on the west side of the shed, over on the far side. I couldn't tell you what track it run in on."

"There was a double track leading out as far as The Shops, or just a little beyond?"

"Yes, sir."

"After you get past The Shops, that double track ends, and then there is a single track on to Harding?"

"Yes, sir."

"Now, on the morning that you left with Mr. Kennedy, you were given these orders, a copy of which Mr. Kennedy read to you: to watch for Engine #281, hauling Train Number One, Engine #282, hold main track, meet Number

Seven, Engine #215, at Harding, that you hold the main track and that you would pass him at Harding?"

"No. It said to meet Number Seven at Harding."

Surprised that Eubank would correct him, the accomplished young lawyer turned his back to the witness stand. Ignoring Eubank's response, he faced the courtroom. "It meant that Number Seven had Engine #215. That is how you would identify the train when you got to Harding?"

"Yes, sir."

Walker spun around. Confronting Eubank face-to-face, he posed another question. "Further down, the orders say Number One has Engine #281. That meant that the Number One train was coming in from Memphis to Nashville into Union Station, and on the front of its engine, against a black background in big brass letters, were the figures '281'—is that right?"

"Yes, sir."

"How big are those letters on an engine? I mean, those figures?"

"They are good, big figures. I couldn't say what size they were. You have to get the mechanic to answer a question like that."

"Eight or ten inches high?"

"I expect something like ten, maybe."

"Ten inches high?"

"I would expect so."

"And they are a yellow or brass color?"

"Yes, sir, they are a brass color."

"And they are right on the front end of the engine; and then up on the headlight in similar numbers, the engine number is painted there in black letters, is that right?"

"Yes, sir. Those numbers are bold enough that anybody riding up at the front should be able to read them from quite a ways away."

Seth Walker retrieved the copy of the train orders he had handed over to William Norvell during the direct examination. Showing the copy of the orders to Eubank, he asked a new question. "Now, Mr. Kennedy had gotten a copy of these orders?"

"Yes, sir."

"The order meant, did it not, unless he had passed Train Number One between the Union Station and The Shops, where this double track ended, that at that point he must stop, didn't it?"

Across the room, William Norvell rose urgently out of his chair. "I want to object to that, if Your Honor pleases. Did Your Honor catch Mr. Walker's question? The order speaks for itself!"

"Yes, sir, I did catch Mr. Walker's question," the judge replied.

Sensing that the judge was not going to rule against his question, Seth Walker went back to his enquiry of Mr. Eubank. "Under operating conditions as they were on that morning, when an engineer who was on an inferior train had failed to meet a superior train that was then due, when he got to the end of the double track, what was the thing for him to do?"

"Stop."

Norvell's voice filled the room again. "Wait a minute! I object to that, unless he qualifies. I take it that it is limited to the rule of what he would know."

"Well, he can answer," the judge ruled. "Of course he would have knowledge of what the custom was, what would be brought about under certain circumstances."

Walker carried on. "Mr. Eubank, I will ask you this question, then. In the same book of rules that Mr. Norvell handed over to you and were asked about earlier, does this appear as Rule Eighty-Three? 'A train must not leave its initial station on any division or junction or pass from double to single track, until it has been ascertained whether all trains due, which are superior or of the same class have arrived or left. A train must not leave its initial station on any division without clearance.'" Walker slammed the rulebook shut. "Is that rule eighty-three?" he asked.

"Yes, sir. That's rule eighty-three."

Opening the book back up to a new page, he showed it to Eubank. "Rule eighty-five is the rule that you and Mr. Kennedy were operating under. It provided this, does it not?" He read aloud, "'When a train must proceed by another train of the same class, it must not go beyond the passing point in advance of the train which is to pass it, unless directed by train order so to do.'" He looked Eubank directly in the eye. "That is rule eighty-five, isn't it?"

"Yes, sir. It is."

Scanning the book, Walker read more. "Rule eighty-seven provides this, does it not? 'Inferior trains'—such as Number Four—'must keep out of the way of superior trains.'"

Agitated, William Norvell interrupted, "Reading the rule into the record does *not* necessarily apply it to Number Four."

Paying no attention to his opponent, Attorney Seth Walker went forward with his cross-examination. "Mr. Eubank. Number Four was an inferior train?"

"Yes, sir."

"Number One was a superior train?"

"Yes, sir."

"Now then, in that connection, I want to read you what purports to be rule eighty-seven into the record." Holding the rulebook open, Walker began. "'Inferior trains must keep out of the way of superior trains in the opposite direction clearing their time as required by rule, and in meeting them must, when practicable, pull into the side at the nearest end. If necessary to pass this point to pull in or back in, the train must be protected as prescribed by rule ninety-nine, unless otherwise provided.'" Walker exhaled slowly. "Now, that is rule eighty-seven, is it not, Mr. Eubank?"

"Yes, it is, sir."

"Let's be clear." Seth Walker spoke slowly. "When you left the Union Station that morning, did you know whether or not Mr. Kennedy had a copy of the order that I have read to you in his hands, and do you know for certain whether or not he read it?"

Eubank squirmed in his seat. All this going back and forth asking and re-asking the same questions was making him dizzy. "Yes, sir, like I said before, he read the order right there in the office. He read it before me. I suppose the operator heard it."

"You also had a copy of the order?"

"Yes, and I read mine back to him."

"I believe you say that just as soon as your train pulled out, you started taking up tickets?"

"Yes."

"What kind of crowd did you have on the train that morning?"

"Well, I never did get through the train. The part of the train I had been through, there was a pretty good bunch. I think there was a pretty good crowd on it."

"The coaches were all full, as far as you know?"

"Yes, sir."

"So, you had a good crowd and were about five minutes late in leaving?"

"I think so. About five minutes late."

"You knew, and other members of the train crew knew, of course, that Number One had not arrived at the time you left?"

"Yes, sir."

"Now, you were asked on direct examination about passing something. Do you know whether that was a train or whether it was just a switch engine backing along there?"

"No, I couldn't tell you what it was. Just the noise of steam was what I was going by. Just the noise."

"When you ran there to look, you didn't see anything? What is your best judgment about what it was?"

"Well, I didn't run to see it. I couldn't get to the window on account of so many people standing at the back of the coach. I couldn't say what it was, Captain, whether it was a switch engine or an engine with cars rolling down there. It was steam that attracted my attention."

"And it was on the same track that Number One was supposed to come in on?"

"Yes, sir."

"Now, Mr. Eubank, you stated on direct examination that when that whatever-it-was passed, you had gotten by while near The Shops, you naturally thought was Number One?"

"Yes, sir. I placed confidence in Uncle Dave that he was looking out for Number One and that it was it that passed by."

"You were in the train with your view cut off from an approaching train such as Number One, so that you could not see the engine number, could you?"

"Not unless I had stopped my work and opened up the platform on the back of the ladies' car and got out where I could see."

"And if you were looking for Number One and had to identify Number One as having Engine #281, you couldn't take up tickets, could you?"

It was good to hear someone else finally say what he'd been saying ever since that terrible morning. He answered with gusto. *"No, sir!"*

"You were busy with tickets. You couldn't perform or attend to any other duties on your train that morning, could you?"

"No, sir! Not between here and the—"

Walker butted in. "Now, prior to July 9, 1918, the day on which this wreck occurred, state whether or not you had failed between Nashville and nearby stations to get through your train in time to take up all the tickets, and whether or not people would get off and take the tickets with them?"

"Well, I can't say for sure what people did with their tickets, but I had failed to get through my train between here and Bellevue, the first regular stop."

"And do you know whether or not people had been bringing back their tickets and asking the company to redeem them?"

"I suppose they had. There was a notice on the bulletin board that said they had."

"With that in mind, is that why you were taking up tickets just as soon as you could?"

William Norvell raised his arm. Waving his hand in the air, he spoke out. "I object to that as inadmissible, Your Honor!"

Judge Neil looked down from the bench. "Overrule the objection."

Irritated with what he believed to be a prejudicial ruling Norvell responded. "I will make a motion to exclude."

Annoyed at the disruption, Walker shook his head as he picked back up where he left off before being interrupted.

"Now, with that in mind, Mr. Eubank, state whether or not you went to Mr. Kennedy prior to that time and had an understanding with him about whether or not he would look out and ascertain whether Number One had always arrived or had not arrived?"

William Norvell rushed to the bench waving a rulebook. "I want to object to this line of testimony on these grounds." Pointing at opposing counsel, he spoke to the judge. "Mr. Walker has kindly furnished me with this rulebook, Your Honor, and I would like to read from it."

Norvell paused, expecting Judge Neil to speak. The judge remained silent, so Norvell continued, "Now, in this rulebook, rule two hundred and four states, 'train orders must be addressed to those who are to execute them, naming the place at which each is to receive his copy.' Rule one hundred and five states, 'the conductor has charge of his train and all persons employed when his instructions conflict with the rule or involve risk, in either of which the engineman will be held alike responsible.'"

Norvell was about to address the issue at the very crux of his client's case, and he carefully chose his next words. "Now, I want to object to that on this ground," he said. "On the grounds that the rules lay a duty alike upon the conductor and the engineer." With precise enunciation, he explained, "The railroad, in defending this suit, cannot contradict its own rules and escape liability by a mode of understanding or a mode of habitual violation of the rules, or anything else. That is the point of my objection."

Judge Neil ruled. "I will let him answer the question under your objection."

Dejected, William Norvell slid back down into his seat.

Confident that the judge would continue to rule in his favor, Seth Walker approached his witness with poise.

"I was asking you, Mr. Eubank—when the objection was made to the question," Walker said as he turned on his heels, making a dramatic gesture at William Norvell. "I was asking you if, while you were engaged in taking up tickets between the Union Station and Shops, where the double tracks ended, whether or not previous to that time and at the time, you had an understanding with Mr. Kennedy, who was on the front end of the engine pulling Number Four, as to whether he would look out and ascertain the arrival of the Number One train?"

"Well, on this morning when we read the orders and come out of the office, I made the remark to him, I said, 'Uncle Dave, Number One must be late this morning.'"

"Now, previous to that time—"

"Other times when I come down the steps, he would call my attention to the crowds filling up the train, and he would say, 'Look yonder at that crowd,' and I says back to him, 'Uncle Dave, you will have to look out for me this morning, I will have my hands full.'"

"How many times had that happened?"

"I couldn't inform you how many times."

"Were you or were you not expecting him to look out, ascertain whether or not Train Number One had arrived, and identify it?"

"Yes, sir, I was depending on him, and the porter, and the flagman, and the fireman. Especially on him, the porter, and the fireman, three old members of the crew. That is where I put my dependence."

"Now, Mr. Eubank, at the place where you passed this something-with-steam, as you termed it. Was it on a curve or a straightaway at that time?"

"It is on a straight line of tracks there."

"What opportunity did the engineer on Train Number Four have to ascertain, at that time and at the place where you passed this something, what it was that passed? Was there anything to obstruct his view at that point?"

"I don't think so," Eubank answered honestly. Shrugging his shoulders, he added, "But I don't know. I wasn't up there to see."

"I will ask you this, then. The track at that point runs straight, doesn't it?"

"Yes, sir. Straight track."

"The engine follows the track and the rails, does it not?"

Wondering if he heard the question right Eubank responded. "The engine ought to follow the track and the rails, sir. If it don't, you will be in mighty bad shape."

A spectator across the room laughed out loud at Eubank's answer. Ignoring the chuckles that followed, Walker maintained his composure. With a steady voice, he went on to ask the next question. "That is right, Mr. Eubank. The engine stays on the rails. The engineer sits in the cab on the lookout right straight ahead?"

"Yes, sir."

"The engineer can look ahead and see what's coming on straight tracks?"

"Yes, sir. He can."

Sitting in the witness stand was uncomfortable and Eubank's neck was tight. He rolled his shoulders back and forth to loosen up his muscles as Seth Walker came at him with even more questions. He couldn't wait for this ordeal to be over.

"What were you doing when this wreck occurred?"

"I was reaching over for a ticket."

"You were not hurt?"

"Well, not to say *hurt*. A suitcase run up against my shin, down there," he said, pointing at his leg. "That was all. When I was reaching over for the ticket, the brakes applied and kind of run me backwards, and I kind of grabbed to the seat and it was all done that quick."

Walker stepped away. Shuffling through some papers and photographs he had left on his chair, he selected a handful. He skimmed over the top paper as he returned to the front of the courtroom.

"This wreck. It happened on a curve and Mr. Kennedy being engineer on Train Number Four, on Engine #282, he would have been on the inside of the that curve, wouldn't he?"

"Yes, sir."

"Now, the engineer on Train Number One, when he was coming around that curve, being on the right hand side, he would be on the blind side of the curve, be on the outside of the curve?"

"Yes, sir."

"So, the boiler on his locomotive would obstruct his view." Flipping through the stack he held, he selected a picture. "I show you a photograph here that has Figure Number Five and words written on it: 'view of track and overhead bridge approached from direction Train Number One was coming in on,' and ask you to state whether or not that correctly represents the situation out there."

Eubank studied the photograph carefully. "What part of the track is this? Is this the west side of the bridge?"

"The notation on the photo said it was taken from the direction that Number One was coming in from. In other words, it is looking toward Nashville."

"It don't show much," Eubank said pointing at the picture. Aiming his finger at a white spot in the middle of the photograph, he pointed to the place where the collision happened. "Here is where we hit. Right back here."

"Back where that steam in the picture is?"

"Yes, sir."

Norvell spoke out. "Mr. Walker, will you mark that spot with a pencil?"

"I already identified it by saying where the steam is Mr. Norvell. The steam is white." Without skipping a beat, he turned the focus back to the witness. "That was a horrible wreck when those two trains came together. Do you assert that to be true, Mr. Eubank?"

"Sure was, horrible. That is what I say."

"The engines were torn all to pieces?"

"Yes, sir."

"Some of the cars were telescoped?"

"Yes, sir."

"The equipment was all but destroyed except three or four coaches?"

"Number One's train wasn't tore up so bad, I don't think, after they passed the baggage car—of course, the two Jim Crow cars, where all the laborers were, wrecked."

"The first three coaches on your train were demolished? They were telescoped? Was the track torn up?"

"I couldn't tell you, Captain. I didn't look much at the track and such as that. There were other things I wanted to look at."

FIG. 1.—GENERAL VIEW OF WRECK.

FIG. 2.—VIEW OF DESTROYED EQUIPMENT.

FIG. 3.—BOILERS OF LOCOMOTIVES 281 (TOP) AND 282 (BOTTOM).

FIG. 4.—VIEW OF CARS AFTER BEING DRAWN APART, SHOWING BAGGAGE CAR AND FIRST COACH OF TRAIN NO. 4 TELESCOPED.

FIG. 5.—VIEW OF TRACK AND OVERHEAD BRIDGE FROM DIRECTION TRAIN NO. 1 WAS TRAVELING.

146

"Now, Mr. Eubank, I wish you would look at a picture here that has Figure Number Four, which says, 'views of cars after being drawn apart, showing baggage car and first coach of Train Number Four being telescoped.' Do you remember that?"

"Yes, that looks to be after the ladies' cars were uncoupled and pulled back toward Nashville."

"I'm going to ask you to file these pictures—which are Figures Four and Five—to be filed respectively as Exhibits One and Two into your testimony." Walker selected another photograph to show Eubank. "Now, I show you a picture labeled Figure Number Two, which has the words 'view of destroyed equipment' written on it, and ask you to state whether or not that correctly represents part of the situation after the wreck?"

"That is the Number One train, I suppose, from the looks it—from the looks of the end of the car there. I just never did look at that side of the wreck but very little."

"Now, I show you on the reverse side of this paper containing Figure Two, two pictures with the words 'boilers of Locomotive #281 at top and boilers of #282 at bottom' and ask you to state whether or not that is correct."

"Yes, sir."

Hearing Eubank's answer, some of the courtroom spectators turned to each other in surprise. There was something wrong with the pictures. Anyone who had been out to the wreck site could see. That Eubank didn't recognize the error in the pictures was confusing to many of the people watching the trial.

One spectator elbowed the side of the man sitting next to him. "Those two pictures are labeled wrong." he whispered, "They have the numbers of the locomotives confused. That's #282 at the top, and #281 is on the bottom. I know that for a fact."

ॐ

Judge Neil called out from the bench. "Court is adjourned until tomorrow morning, October 22, 1920, at nine o'clock." He banged his gavel and the courtroom stirred again with activity.

After sitting still and being interrogated for almost four hours, Shorty Eubank couldn't wait to get outside and breathe some fresh air. He stepped out of the witness stand as soon as he heard the bang of the judge's gavel. He rushed out of the crowded courtroom before many others in the room had even risen to their feet.

Unlike Eubank, the men of the jury lingered inside the courtroom. They hadn't been allowed to speak to each other since the noon break was over, and now that court was adjourned, they huddled together to discuss the afternoon proceedings. One juror, sympathetic to Shorty Eubank, spoke up. "If Eubank had an agreement with the rest of the train crew to watch out for the incoming train, I don't think he should be faulted for not watching the tracks."

"But that wasn't the rule of the road," replied another juror, adding, "But it does seem unfair to fault him when he was busy taking up tickets like he was told to do."

A third man piped in. "I'm just glad that we were sworn to sit on a civil trial and that this ain't a murder trial like that train engineer and his fireman went through last summer up in Indiana." He kept talking as the twelve tired men made their way toward the door. "I read that the jury in that trial deadlocked. I sure hope that don't happen with us."

The case he referred to was in regard to the wreck that had happened in the early morning hours of June 22, 1918, just seventeen days before the train wreck out at Dutchman's Curve. Train engineer Alonzo Sargent was operating a troop train on the Michigan Central Railroad. At approximately 4:00 a.m., Sargent drove through two automatic signals and past warnings posted by a flagman on a twenty-six car circus train that was occupying the tracks in front of him. The circus train had made an emergency stop. After completely missing the warnings, Engineer Sargent plowed into the four rear wooden sleeping cars. At least eighty-six circus performers and roustabouts were killed in the crash. Immediately after the crash, Engineer Alonzo Sargent and his fireman, Gustave Klauss, were criminally charged with eighty-six counts of murder.

With two train wrecks in the news causing such a huge loss of life and happening in such a short span of time, people in Nashville were very interested in comparisons between the circus train wreck and the murder trial that followed.

Twelve days after the train wreck out at Dutchman's Curve happened, the *Chicago Defender* ran an article calling the train wreck an act of "wholesale murder"—but no authorities in Nashville took the charge seriously, and no criminal charges against the surviving train crew members were ever filed.

Now, after a full day of legal proceedings, it seemed clear from the facts that the train wreck out at Dutchman's Curve was a terrible accident that was the result of more than one error. The jury was going to be hard-pressed to find the NC&StL Railway completely blameless in causing the train wreck. It was apparent to the jury that the railroad company, the government agency in charge of running it and at least at least one employee other than David Kennedy played a part in making the terrible accident happen.

Chapter Twenty

Fallen leaves rustled across the sidewalk in front of the Davidson County Courthouse on the morning of October 22, 1920, as a gentle breeze blew across the Nashville Public Square. Shortly before nine, a bevy of witnesses, jurors, and spectators turned up at the courthouse for day two of the Kennedy lawsuit trial.

Inside the courtroom, Railroad Attorney Seth Walker restarted his cross-examination of Shorty Eubank. Holding some documents in his hand, he approached the former conductor.

"Mr. Eubank, this order that I have here was given to you, a copy of which you say was given to Mr. Kennedy, the engineer, was what is known in the rulebook among railroad men as Order Form Nineteen?"

"Yes, sir."

"I want to ask you to file his order, Form Nineteen in its original form, as Exhibit Number Five to your testimony."

"I will."

"This other thing that I show you, this book of rules, is the same book or one exactly like it about which you were interrogated yesterday by Mr. Norvell and myself, is it not?"

"Yes, it is, sir."

"I will ask you to file that as Exhibit Number Six to your testimony."

Walker turned the copy of the order and the book over to a court clerk as he probed Eubank for more information. "Now, in what way did the engineer have to identify Train Number One?"

"By the engine number given in the order, Captain."

"Prior to July 9th, 1918, the morning of this wreck, state whether or not many times previous that similar orders had been given to you and to Mr. Kennedy, the engineer, with reference to the meeting point of the Number One."

Shrugging his shoulders, Eubank answered. "Well, I can't remember, Mr. Walker, about how many orders we would get about Number One."

"Previous to July ninth, Mr. Eubank?"

"That is what I say, Captain. I can't remember exactly."

"Hadn't you been given orders before about the engine number that Number One had?"

"Some mornings we would get an order about Number One, and nearly every morning we got an order about Number Seven."

"About where to meet Number Seven?"

"Yes, sir, every other morning, not every morning."

Springing from his seat, Attorney William Norvell called out. "These gentlemen have possession of the orders, and they are the best evidence, Your Honor!"

Judge Neil nodded his head in agreement. "Yes, sir, they are the best evidence."

"I am not objecting right now," he said. Norvell sat back down.

Seth Walker moved towards the judge's bench. "We *have* got the orders. I will withdraw the question, Your Honor."

He reverted back to Eubank. "When your train was on time, Mr. Eubank, when Number Four was on time and when Number One was on time, between what points would Train Number Four pass Train Number One?"

"Well, you say, we would meet anywhere from the terminal depot to The Shops, somewhere in there."

"In other words, if Train Number One was on time, which was due to arrive at the station at 7:10 a.m., and Train Number Four was on time, that was due to leave the station at 7:00 a.m., those respective trains would pass each other between the Union Station and The Shops, the point where the double track ends?"

"Yes, sir, on that time."

"Train Number Four, when on time, arrived at The Shops at 7:08, did it not?"

"I think that is the time, there. Yes, sir."

"Now, what were the rule and customs with reference to whether or not if Train Number Four had not passed Train Number One between the Union Station and The Shops, as to where Number Four was to go, either to go past The Shops or stop there?"

"We stop there."

"Now, in case you failed to pass Number One between Union Station and The Shops, in order to get by The Shops, what was necessary to have done?"

"Stop and go to The Shops, and see if they will give you another order against Number One."

"From whom would you get the order?"

"We would get it from the telegraph operator at The Shops. He would get it from the train dispatcher at the depot."

"Mr. Eubank, the engineer and fireman who were in charge of Engine #281 that was pulling Train Number One were killed, were they not?"

"Yes, sir. They were killed."

Finished with the cross-examination of Shorty Eubank, Seth Walker returned to his seat. William Norvell stood to begin his redirect examination of the witness.

"Mr. Eubank, Mr. Walker asked you about stopping at other times in the past and getting orders at The Shops against Number One, that is, at the tower at The Shops."

"Yes, sir."

"I will ask you whether or not in those other instances when you had stopped at The Shops, the signal arm there, was that clear?"

"I can't tell you, that morning."

"Sir?"

"I can't tell you anything about it that morning."

"I am not asking you about that morning. I'm asking you about the other times when you stopped. When the signal arm is up, that is a clear signal?"

"Yes, sir. It's supposed to be."

"What does it mean when it's down?"

"Down? That is a stop signal."

"I will ask you whether or not on a previous morning, when Number One was late and your train had stopped at the tower and you and the engineer had gotten other orders against Number One, if those instances, the stop signal hadn't been there?"

"Yes, sir, if it was standing against us then I would go over after orders."

"Of course, on this particular morning you were in your train and you couldn't see what the signal was, and those other mornings, you got out to get your orders and could see?"

"Whenever the train would come to a stop I would quit my work and go to see what the delay would be."

"Now, what does that rule mean about the train register—does that mean a sheet that the operator would keep, or does it mean in addition thereto a stopping point where the conductor or engineer would keep, or does it mean in addition thereto a stopping point where the conductor or engineer or both have to stop their train and see whether another train has passed and examine the register and sign it? In other words, to make myself clear, when you leave Nashville, there's a train register there?"

"Yes, sir."

"You examine that, and you also sign it?"

"How is that?"

"Don't you sign the train register here at Nashville when you leave?"

"Yes, sir, we register out."

"And that shows what other trains have come in or left prior to you?"

It was painful for Eubank to recall the minute details of the job he'd done for decades. Recounting his past duties reminded Eubank of how important his former job had been and how far he fallen. Downcast, he answered. "Yes. That register shows the arrivals and the departures."

"Now, I say, you have stated what was at The Shops, but in addition thereto, it was at a place where you gentlemen, I mean by 'you gentlemen' you and the engineer, had to register in or out unless there was a stop signal?"

"At The Shops, Captain?"

"Yes."

"No, sir, we didn't register in and out of there."

William Norvell paced in front of the witness stand. "Mr. Eubank!"

Norvell stopped moving. The upcoming question was important to his case, and he asked it with a stern voice. "Mr. Eubank, state for me whether or not, particularly when your train is crowded so that the conductor might be a little extra busy, if it is not the custom for the flagman to do any looking out for the conductor for trains passing and so forth?"

"Well, the flagman looks out..."

Seth Walker's voice sounded abruptly throughout the room. "Objected to by the defendants as immaterial under the allegations of the declaration!"

"Overruled!"

Satisfied with the judge's ruling, Norvell urged Eubank to answer the question.

"Please, go on."

"I say, the flagman looks out at stations to get the passengers off and get them on." Eubank glanced at the faces of the railroad bosses sitting on the defense side of the room. They appeared to be pleased with his answer.

"And just as you stated yesterday, the engineer gets his order and shows that to the fireman, and under your rule, the other party to whom that order is addressed, namely the conductor, gives his copy or shows it to the flagman, under the rule, doesn't he?"

"Yes, sir."

"And the flagman is there to assist the conductor?"

"Yes, sir."

"In seeing that the orders are carried out and making a report to him, isn't that correct?"

"No, they don't always make a report to the conductor."

"I understand they don't always. The flagman certainly didn't report in this case. I am asking you now, is it part of his duty when you give him a train order—" Norvell's voice was cut short as Walker interrupted.

"Objection! I object because the rule is the best evidence."

"Objection sustained!"

Unhappy with the ruling, William Norvell went back to his redirect. "Reforming my question, Mr. Eubank, isn't it the custom, and particularly, I will say, when the train is crowded so that the conductor has extra arduous duties, for the flagman to be on the lookout for the passage of trains and other things to see that the train orders are observed?"

"I think it is the custom for us all to lookout when we are crowded that way, for any member of the crew."

"I understand, Mr. Eubank, that you have covered the engineer, I am not talking to you about that—"

Tired of being talked down to, Eubank interrupted the lawyer in exasperation. "I am talking to *you* about the *facts*, sir."

"The flagman, I suppose, will take the order and read it and lookout for the safety train?"

"Of course. He is a member of the crew."

"And if I understand you, it is the custom particularly when the conductor is a little overworked for the flagman and the other members of the crew to be on the lookout for the observation and following of the train orders."

Seth Walker shot out of his seat. "Defendants object to this method of examination, Your Honor! Counsel is leading his own witness."

"Overruled," the judge responded. "The witness may answer the question."

Eubank complied. "Yes, sir. We are all on the lookout."

William Norvell steered clear of the subject of the missing flagman and followed a different line of reasoning.

"Mr. Eubank, when you were passing this other train or engine, approximately how fast was your own train going?"

"Well, I can't hardly say, Captain. I was busy in my train and I didn't pay any attention as to what speed we picked up at all."

"You were still, so to speak, in the yards?"

"Yes, sir, we were in the yard limits."

"To refresh your recollection, Mr. Eubank, your train hadn't gotten to a speed of over fifteen or twenty miles an hour when it got to that point."

"I can't say one way or the other what speed we were running up that hill, I was busy in my train. Sometimes we would get pretty near stopped for the signal to go ahead again, but we usually run something like twenty miles an hour along there."

"You have no recollection of going along there, on this occasion, faster than that?"

"No, sir, or no other occasion along there, going up that hill."

"Now, Mr. Eubank, you stated that you showed your order to the porter. There is nothing in the rules about showing it to your porter, is there?"

"I didn't show it to the porter, I read it to him."

"There is nothing in the printed rules of your company requiring you to read the order to your porter, is there?"

Noticeably bothered, Eubank answered the question. "I don't know that there is," he said.

"I pass you the rulebook. Look at Rule Two Hundred and Eleven, which shows to whom the orders are to be shown by the engineer and the conductor, and see if it says anything about the porter, and see if you recall any other part of the rule that shows that?"

Eubank halfheartedly looked down at the book. Whoever wrote the rulebook didn't know the deceased railroad porter George Hall—but Eubank did. He had known him to be an able railroader, and Eubank was confident that the trust he had placed in him was well deserved.

Train conductors had more authority than any other person on the train, even more than the engineer, and it rankled the former conductor's pride that longstanding customs he established when he was in charge of overseeing the Number Four train were now being called into question just because they didn't exactly line up with the way things were supposed to be done according to the rulebook.

"Now, Mr. Eubank, it had been your custom to show your order to your porter, hadn't it, just as you did that morning?"

"I read them to him every morning, yes, sir."

"Furthermore, wasn't it your custom, since he was a member of the train crew, for the porter, particularly when the conductor was overworked, as you said you were that morning—"

"How is that, sir?" Eubank asked, cutting in on the lawyer's question.

"I will ask you whether or not it was not the custom, particularly when the conductor was overworked with a big crowd, as you said you had that morning—"

"Well, Captain..."

"Wait a minute. Let me finish my question. I say, was it not the custom particularly when the conductor was overworked, and there was a big crowd on the train, as you say there was that morning, for the porter to receive or to see a copy of the train order and to be on the lookout for the passage of trains and other things so that they might be clear?"

"It was the custom with me to read the train order to my porter. How it was among the other men, I don't know. I didn't know and I couldn't tell you whether or not the train was going to be crowded when I read the order to him. I didn't know how many was going to be on there."

"I didn't mean the reading of the order, Mr. Eubank, you never caught my question. Here is the question: if on occasions, particularly when the train was crowded and the conductor was overworked, not that you showed him the train order, but wasn't it the custom for the porter also to lookout for passing trains to see that train orders were observed, and didn't you depend on him that morning because he was part of the train crew?"

"I depended on all the employees to all the time to help me lookout for everything . I especially depended on the two working at front end of the train."

Shorty Eubank stayed put in the witness stand as William Norvell retreated back to his seat. Seth Walker stepped up to the front of the courtroom to begin his second cross-examination of the witness.

"You were asked about this particular morning with reference to the signal at The Shops, whether there was a proceed or whether there was a stop signal. You don't know how it was on this particular morning, do you?"

"No, sir."

"When the signal arm is standing straight, vertical then means a proceed signal?"

"Yes, sir."

"And when it's standing at forty-five degrees, that is a stop signal, is that right?"

"Yes, sir."

"Now you are not governed by the signals at The Shops as to whether to proceed and go by, are you?"

"Well, whenever we went by, if I happened to be where I could see the signal any time, that it would always be clear."

"You were governed by the train orders that were given to you, and by the superiority of the trains, weren't you?"

"Yes, sir, that is what we are governed by."

"Now, assuming that when you left Nashville to The Shops, you saw a proceed signal there, and while you were going with your train order, the position of that signal, even if it was at proceed in view of your train order—that didn't give you any right to go on out of The Shops, did it?" Walker rephrased. "In other words, unless the engineer knew that Train Number One had arrived and had gotten past The Shops and had gotten off of the single track, no matter *what* position the signal at The Shops was standing at, he didn't have any right to go by, did he, under the rule?"

"No, sir, he didn't have any right to go by."

"In other words, unless the engineer knew that Train Number One had arrived and had gotten past The Shops, and had gotten off of the single track, no matter *what* position the signal was standing at The Shops, he didn't have the right to go by, did he, under the rule?"

"No, sir."

"Now, Mr. Eubank, Train Number Four was operated, as I believe you stated, by train orders. Is that a fact?"

"Yes, sir."

"Yes, sir, we had to have order to get any further."

Seth Walker gestured toward Shorty Eubank and addressed the judge. "I have no more questions for this witness, Your Honor."

Judge Neil looked down at Shorty Eubank and said the words the conductor had been longing to hear for two days. "You are excused, sir."

Chapter Twenty-One

With Mr. Eubank finally off the witness stand, Norvell turned the next witness over to the other lawyer representing Mary Kennedy in this case, Malachi Bryan.

The courtroom proceedings the day before had taken a toll on Mary Kennedy. She'd remained intent on Mr. Eubank's mannerisms the whole time he was testifying, and she was fatigued. She was visibly exhausted, and Mr. Bryan felt sorry for her. He gave her a gentlemanly pat on the back as he passed by her chair, and made his way to the front of the courtroom to interrogate the new witness.

Mr. Bryan asked his first question. "You are Squire Patrick J. Geary?"

The man on the witness on the stand was distraught. He had been very good friends with David Kennedy for many years and he disliked the thought of discussing his friends character in public. Clinching the sides of the chair, he answered. "Yes, I am Patrick Geary."

"What business are you in, Mr. Geary?"

"Retail shoe merchant."

"Connected with what firm?"

"The Kuhn, Cooper, and Geary Company."

"Were you acquainted with David Campbell Kennedy?"

"Yes, sir.

"How long had you known Mr. Kennedy?"

"I have been knowing him for over thirty years."

"Were you very intimately acquainted with him?"

He hung his head and answered reluctantly. "Very intimately acquainted with him."

"What business was he engaged in while you knew him?"

"Locomotive engineer."

"Mr. Geary, please speak up and tell the court and the jury what character of man was he, in regard to his physical activities."

"He was a very good man, very active."

"Was he a fleshy man or a thin man, or how would you describe him?"

"He wasn't a fleshy man, I would safely say he was a man that weighed about one hundred and sixty pounds, along about that. I don't know his exact weight, but he was a medium-built man."

"What do you know about his habit of exercise, walking or anything like that?"

"Well, he was very active, he could walk. We used to play cards every other night or so, and he would get out the window in the back and go walk. He would try to play games, such as baseball. He liked to play baseball."

"Was he a ball enthusiast?"

"Very much so. He used to go to every game he could go to."

"How long had it been since you saw him or talked to him before his life was taken in the wreck?"

"Let's see," Geary said, as he carefully considered the question. "I think that wreck happened on a Tuesday morning. Yes, I believe it was a Tuesday morning. I don't know the exact day I saw him last, but I guess I saw him less than a week before he was killed. You see, I never got to see him on Saturday nights because my store was always open for business then."

Mr. Bryan gestured toward the jury, including them in his next question. "Can you tell us of anything you did for Mr. Kennedy or assisted him in that brought you into personal contact with him?"

Nodding his head, Geary answered. "He used to come in to the store and transact business. I used to pay up his premium, life insurance for him, and he done several acts of charity. He would leave money in my possession to give to those in need. He was a very charitable man."

Hearing that David Kennedy took care of the poor sat well with the spectators watching the trial, and sounds and nods of approval spread throughout the room.

Bryan circled the front of the courtroom, stopping in front of the row where Mary Kennedy and her daughters sat.

He called out his next question to Geary. "So, you saw David Kennedy frequently, then?"

"He was in the store every trip. Every trip, he usually would come in."

Moving back toward the witness stand, Bryan looked Geary in the eye. "After this wreck happened on the day of the ninth of July, did you visit the wreck?"

"Yes, sir. I went out to see about Mr. Kennedy's affairs."

"What time did you get there?"

"I must have got there along about, well, when I heard it, it was along about between eight thirty and nine o'clock."

"Was there any search made while you were there for the body of Mr. Kennedy?"

"We were all looking to see what we could do, I was helping to get the people straightened out, finding them some place to go. But I was there to find Mr. Kennedy. That was my object for going."

"You assisted to relieve the distress?"

"Yes, sir. I helped in several cases."

Bryan softened a bit, and asked his next question in a kinder tone. "While you were there, was the body of Mr. Kennedy discovered?"

"Yes, sir. We found it under the machinery, under a wheel. His face was burned so bad we could barely recognize the features. We didn't know for sure until they pulled him up a bit, and we found some papers and his watch in his pocket."

"Who acquainted his family, his wife, of his death? Who was it did that, notified his wife?"

Looking at the three Kennedy women, Mr. Geary sighed sadly and answered. "I did. I was the one that told his wife. It was me that told her of his death."

"How well acquainted are you with Mrs. Kennedy?"

"I'm very well acquainted. I've been knowing Mrs. Kennedy for the same length of time that I knew him. Thirty years."

"What is the condition of her health since the accident?"

"Well, at the time of the accident, she had some nervous trouble because of the wreck , she was ill for some time, but her health at present is some better."

"Mr. Geary, referring to Mr. Kennedy's health and activity, how did he compare with other men of the same age, ordinarily?"

"I would consider he would be a much more active man than other people at his age. I can compare him with my father-in-law. They were about the same age, and my father-in-law is a very disabled man and unable to go out and about, but Mr. Kennedy could."

"Was he active mentally as well as physically?"

"Yes, sir, he was."

"Thank you Mr. Geary. I have no more questions for this witness." Bryan left the front of the courtroom as Seth Walker briskly made his way to the witness stand.

Walker only had one question he wanted answered. "Do you know how long Mr. Kennedy had been drawing a pension, Mr. Geary?"

"You mean from the government?"

"Yes, from the United States government?"

"No, sir, I don't know. We used to cash his pension checks for him. I guess he must have been drawing it for a quite a while."

"How long?"

"I have been in business about fifteen years, and I have cashed them possibly about that length of time for him."

"So, he has been drawing a pension for as long as fifteen years then?"

"Yes, sir, between twelve and fifteen years."

"I am finished with this witness, Your Honor."

Chapter Twenty-Two

Charles B. Glenn was a no-nonsense man of numbers. Unlike the witnesses who had testified before him, Mr. Glenn didn't know David Kennedy, and he wasn't part of the train crew or a wreck witness.

He had no personal opinions to offer in court on this day. His testimony would be dictated by a ledger of dollars and cents, not by his feelings for the departed or his understanding of railroad rules and regulations. Unruffled by the formality of the court, he took his seat in the witness stand and calmly waited for attorney William Norvell to ask his first question.

"Mr. Glenn, you are paymaster for the NC&StL Railway. Is that correct?"

"Yes, sir."

"You had charge of the payrolls during the operations in the war?"

"Yes, sir."

"Mr. Glenn, have you made up from your records a statement showing the earnings of the deceased, David Campbell Kennedy, from the road or the operating authorities of the road for the last ten years?"

"Yes, sir. That is, ten years prior to his death."

"Will you kindly produce that statement?"

"I will." Removing a handwritten list of figures from his vest pocket, he unfolded it and displayed it to the court.

"What did Mr. Kennedy earn in June of 1918, the month before he died?"

Without looking at the paper, he answered. "My list doesn't include 1918. I was told to make a list up to January 1918. What I have on my list is up to December of 1917 inclusive. I could have made it through 1918, but that is not what I was asked to do, and that is the reason I didn't make it." The paymaster paused. Addressing William Norvell with indifference, he rebuked the lawyer for not being precise about what he wanted. "If you wanted his records up through 1918, I could have made it without trouble. You just should have asked me to."

Ignoring the reprimand, Norvell asked a different question. "What did Mr. Kennedy earn in December of 1917?"

Taking a pair of spectacles out of the same pocket that he removed the list from, he slipped them on and quickly scanned the list.

"$253.60." he said.

"In November?"

"$253.60."

"In October?"

"$252.00."

"Now, Mr. Glenn, the paper you have in your hand shows his wages from the railroad or operating authorities of the railroad for the ten years preceding January 1st, 1918."

Joining the plaintiff attorney doing the questioning at the front of the courtroom, Walker addressed the witness. "Will you kindly file that list as Exhibit Number One to your testimony, Mr. Glenn?"

"Yes, sir. I will."

Norvell interrupted. "If it is agreeable to counsel on the other side—I don't want to bother you unnecessarily, Mr. Glenn—I would like for you to prepare a statement showing the earnings of Mr. Kennedy from January 1st, 1918 to July 9th, 1918."

"I can't give you to July 9th, sir, we only go by months. The payroll only shows from month to month."

"Say, then, through July. As a matter of fact, he died July 9th, 1918. We will say, then, from January 1st, 1918 to August 1st, 1918."

Walker spoke up. "Have the statement include up to July 1st. He died on July 9th."

Tired of splitting hairs with the defense, William Norvell offered a compromise. "Anyway, Mr. Glenn, lets put it this way. Please prepare a statement showing how much Mr. Kennedy earned from month to month starting in January of 1918 until he got off your payroll. That will catch it. Then, with permission of opposing counsel, will you kindly send it up here by a messenger and let it be filed as Exhibit Number Two of your testimony?"

"Yes, sir. I can send that up in a short time."

⌇

In 1920, the NC&StL Railway had reached its height of its operations. It was a twelve-hundred-and-fifty-mile road comprised of five divisions. the Nashville, Paducah and Memphis, Chattanooga, Atlanta, and the Huntsville divisions. Each division had its own superintendent in charge of controlling all railroad operations within the division, as well as hiring, training, and managing the division's personnel.

Watson G. Templeton was superintendent of the Nashville division of the NC&StL Railway. Weeks before this trial began; William Norvell had subpoenaed him to appear in court. Mr. Templeton was a no-show the first day of the trial—when he was supposed to appear —and on this Friday, when he finally turned up to testify, it caused a stir in the courtroom.

Norvell was pleased to have the superintendent sitting in the witness stand. Although Templeton was an involuntary witness, Mr. Norvell was certain that the railroad man's testimony would be instrumental in helping the plaintiffs win this case. He greeted the witness with enthusiasm.

"Mr. Templeton, in your capacity as Superintendent of the Nashville Division of the Nashville Chattanooga, and Saint Louis Railway, you had served on you a subpoena *duces tecum* to bring certain records to court. Will you kindly produce the record showing how long Sinclair, the flagman on Number Four on the morning of July 9, 1918, had been employed by the road, and then how long had he been on this northwestern run?"

Seth Walker shouted across the courtroom, stopping Mr. Templeton before he could answer "I object! It is immaterial how long Sinclair had been in the employ of the railway. There is no count in the declaration charging negligence against this man."

"I can cure that objection, I think, if that is really their objection, Your Honor." Norvell said. "In the testimony of Eubank, it seemed to be the tendency to show that there was no duty on him at all on account of being busy out there with all those tickets. Therefore, I want to ask leave of the court to amend the declaration so as to allege, may it please the court, negligence on behalf of the flagman, under those circumstances, in not watching out for and observing whether or not Number One had passed and in failing to report to the conductor as the train pulled down that it had not passed. Also, to allege negligence of the road in allowing the train to become so crowded that the conductor could not perform his duties under the rules in the proper observance and safety of passengers and other employees on the train, and in not substituting the flagman to act in his behalf at that point." Ignoring his witness sitting on the stand, Norvell argued his case before the judge. "I would like to make those two amendments to the declaration. The gentleman comes with the proposition that under this custom and circumstances and so forth, say, he could not be expected to comply. I think in that case, I am entitled to that amendment on behalf of the flagman, because under the rule, the conductor passed his order to the flagman and the engineer to the fireman. Now if the principal upon whom the obligation was laid was so busy, and his train was so crowded, then that threw the direct duty onto his subordinate. And the road further, under such circumstances, was negligent in providing this conductor, so engaged that he couldn't perform his duties under the rule, with a green and inexperienced flagman."

Barging in on the argument, Seth Walker stated his side of the case. "I thought we settled this question of amendment when the trial started out, Your Honor. Mr. Eubank was the plaintiff's witness, and because he developed this custom existing between the engineer and himself, as Mr. Eubank testified, that is no fault of the defendants. The two men developed that by their own witness. Now, Mr. Norvell seeks at this late hour to amend the declaration so as to make an allegation of negligence with reference to the flagman. Now, we don't know where Sinclair is. He is not in the employ of the company. We can't find him, and we can't get him here. It looks to me, at this late hour, unfair when we have proceeded with the trial of the case on the theories laid in the declaration without any notice from them that this was going to happen, and without any preparation to meet it to permit them to amend the declaration."

Courtroom shenanigans were nothing new to Judge Neil. He had presided over the Circuit Court of Davidson County for more almost ten years, and was well-versed in the antics of trial lawyers. On this day, he calmly and impassively listened as William Norvell and Seth Walker battled against each other.

"The gentleman and I have both practiced law here for a few years," Norvell stated, nodding his head toward Seth Walker. "Your Honor knows that amendments are liberal. May it please the court, of course, this was developed through my witness, yes, but in this case, and it many times happens in cases like of this kind, you have to summon the defendant's witnesses to prove your case. Mr. Sinclair is the defendant's witness, and he is not here. Mr. Sinclair had the duty to approach the conductor to have the train flagged down, and their own man, Eubank, who has been in the defendants employ for two years or more since this accident occurred, and who they had a perfect right to talk to—and who they have evidently talked to, and properly did they talk to him—they knew he would testify that the flagman didn't approach him. And now, may it please the court, we also have looked for Mr. Sinclair, and in examining Mr. Eubank on the stand yesterday, I thought possibly he could locate Mr. Sinclair and saw only then that he had no information on his whereabouts. The gentleman said it is unfair to allege that this flagman was green. He had notice last term what the subpoena *duces tecum* contained. The other allegation is that, in a crowded train like this, where they say the conductor couldn't perform his duties, then it was negligence on the part of this flagman in not notifying the conductor to flag down the train. Now, there is not one iota of proof that this flagman did notify the conductor, and this man on the stand, Mr. Templeton—who is as much their witness as he is my witness, as he is in their employ, but technically, I subpoenaed him here—would testify that the flagman did not approach the conductor."

Norvell paused, taking a deep breath. He humbly lowered his head and he beseeched the judge to see things his way. "I say, Your Honor, that this is a fair and proper amendment, and is based upon written records in their possession which they are producing, and upon their statements of men in their employ here on the stand, and I want to insist upon this: that it is fair."

Seth Walker chimed in. "In reference to this matter, Your Honor, this accident happened in 1918, and that goes into the question of shortage of equipment and personnel on account of the war, the powder plant, and other things, and it develops a great big thing. There were many green men working that day. I say, at this late day, when the plaintiff had an opportunity to make this amendment before the trial—in fact, according to Mr. Norvell, they issued a subpoena to have these records brought here at the last term of court, and when they knew at that hour these matters, that with that knowledge that they have had all these months that certainly they ought not now, after getting us into the train, to come along and make these amendments."

Judge Neil stopped the argument. He had heard enough. He pounded his gavel and ruled.

"Let the amendment be made. Go ahead with the witness."

Gratified by the judge's ruling William Norvell, returned to his witness with confidence. "Mr. Templeton, please read your record that I asked for showing when Sinclair came into the employ of your road. What was he doing when he first ran on this train?"

He worked on June 28th, 1918, and June 29th, July 1st, and July 2nd, going over the road posting himself on the local conditions. He claimed, as I recall, that he had been in the railroad service for several years, but he was not familiar with this road. I think he said he came to us from some road down in West Tennessee."

"That's hearsay, of course, Mr. Templeton, but go ahead."

"On July 5th, he was placed on the regular extra brakeman list, to be called first in and first out with the other men, and on the 6th and 7th and 8th, he was used as a regular brakeman. On the 9th, he was called for service and went out as flagman on Number Four which was wrecked, and he has not worked for the company since."

"In other words, your records show that he commenced work June 28th, 1918?"

"He was posting at that time. He went on as a regular full-fledged employee having passed the regular examination on July 5th."

"And then on July 6th, your record shows that he was a regular employee, is that correct?"

"Yes, sir. He was added to the regular list July 5th, subject to be called at any time."

"On the 6th and 7th you have got him as a brakeman. What does that mean?"

"It means he was on a freight train."

"Does the record show on what division?"

"This one."

"The division that this accident happened on?"

"Yes, sir."

"Do your records then show that on July 9th, he was a passenger-train flagman on Number Four?"

"Yes, sir."

"In looking at the summary of your record that you produced earlier, it said that he worked as a brakeman, five hours on the 6th, four hours on the 7th, and one hour on the 8th. Is that correct?"

"No, sir, that is the number of overtime hours he received in addition to the day."

"Mr. Templeton, you say that Mr. Sinclair had no further connection with the road after July 9th?"

"Well, we carried him on the seniority roster for some time, and tried to get him to come on back and work, and he wouldn't do it. He never worked any since." Hesitating, he looked to the jury as he qualified his answer. "He could have worked if he wanted to."

It seemed unlikely to most of the spectators sitting in the courtroom that the railroad company would allow the inept flagman to keep his job after the accident, and murmurs of disbelief rippled through the room.

Encouraged by the reaction of the audience, Mr. Norvell quickly smiled at Mary Kennedy to let her know that this testimony was going her way as he asked his next question. "How long did you carry him on your seniority roster?"

"He is still on there. We tried to get him to come back to work after the accident, but I believe he said he was sick. I wrote him a letter later, but the letter was returned 'not delivered', and I haven't heard any further from him since."

"When was the last time you contacted him?"

"I wrote him on August 29th to ask him to come back to work. The letter was returned to me on November 4th, 1918. That was the last of it."

The sound of church bells ringing in the noon hour drifted through an open window in the room. William Norvell waited for them to stop. Addressing the court, he

174

ended his inquiry of Mr. Templeton. "I have no more questions at this time, Your Honor."

Seth Walker stepped forward. Directing emphasis away from the flagman Sinclair, he changed the course of the interrogation. "Mr. Templeton, the railroads were taken over by the government on the 29th of December 1917, were they not?"

"Yes, sir. They were."

"In July 1918, on July 9th, there was a powder plant in operation here about twelve or fifteen miles from Nashville, wasn't there?"

"They were constructing one out there before that, and probably had some of it in operation then."

"They employed about twenty-five to thirty thousand men out there, didn't they?"

"That was my understanding."

"Did they take any men away from the railway system here or not?"

"Why it took a great many away, but the increased business at that time had more effect though than the actual taking of the men away from the road."

"I am coming to that later. But at any rate, the high wages paid out there did take considerable railroad men away?"

"Yes."

"What was the amount of traffic going on, on July 9th, 1918?"

"It was double the amount of ordinary freight traffic, and I expect the passenger traffic was about double also."

"What was the condition of the NC&StL and other railways at that time with reference to the want? What was the lack of equipment on account of the immense amount of traffic?"

"We were very short of equipment."

"Due to what?"

"Due to increased volume of business."

"What was done with passenger coaches and such equipment with reference to the transportation of soldiers at that time?"

"They were sent to various cantonments or military headquarters to move troops as they were ordered by the government."

"Railroads everywhere felt the same lack?"

"I suppose so."

Knowing that the men of the jury well remembered the lack suffered by both individuals and businesses during the war years, Walker gave them a moment to reflect on those times before he began a different line of questioning.

Chapter Twenty-Three

Outside the courthouse on a marbled portico, Anna Mae Kennedy sat on a bench with her mother and younger sister. Sharing a sandwich, the three women enjoyed their lunch as they waited for court to resume. They were relieved that at last Mr. Templeton was off the witness stand.

His cross-examination had been tedious. Seth Walker had repeated almost every question asked by William Norvell during the direct examination, and had kept the witness on the stand long past noon. Another reason they were happy to see Mr. Templeton go was the fact that he was not a friendly witness. Even though he had been called in by the plaintiffs, Mr. Templeton was not sympathetic to their cause in the least, and the Kennedy women were glad he was gone and a friendly witness was about to take the stand.

Mrs. Kennedy was fond of children and young people, and the next scheduled witness, Dr. William McCabe, had always been one of her favorites. She had had known him ever since he was a little boy, and was very proud of him when he announced his decision to go to college and study medicine.

He had been away at war when the train wreck happened. He didn't get sent back to Nashville until months after the Armistice was signed. Once home, he was quick to advocate the cause of Mrs. Kennedy and had unhesitatingly agreed to speak up for her in court.

Brushing sandwich crumbs from the front of their dresses, the Kennedy women got up from the bench and went back inside the courthouse. Seeing that William McCabe was already in the courtroom, they hurried to their seats and eagerly waited for court to recommence.

ॐ

With a relaxed tone in his voice, Malachi Bryan asked his new witness the first question. "You are Dr William M. McCabe?"

"Yes, sir."

"Where were you graduated from?"

"At Vanderbilt."

"How long ago?"

"1913."

"Have you been a practicing physician ever since?"

"Yes, sir."

"Have you ever held any official position as a physician in the city of Nashville?"

"Yes, sir. I was the superintending surgeon at Nashville City Hospital for some years."

"Were you acquainted with David Campbell Kennedy and his family?"

"Yes, sir. I had known him all my life."

"And are you acquainted with Mrs. Kennedy?"

"Yes, sir."

"Were you in Nashville at the time of the railroad accident in which Mr. Kennedy lost his life?"

"No, sir. I was in France, in the army."

"What was your rank, doctor?"

"I was a captain, and promoted to a major in the medical corps."

"Doctor, tell the court and the jury, if you please, since you knew Mr. Kennedy, whether he was a man of physical activity or not."

"Yes, Mr. Kennedy was a man of physical activity. Very active."

"Doctor, it has been showed that he was seventy-two years of age at the time of his death. Did he look that age?"

"No, sir."

"How long before his death was it that you saw him last?"

"I saw him just before going to France in 1917."

"What was the condition of his health at the time that you saw him?"

"Very good. He was up and around actively. I had never known him to be ill."

Bryan quickly brandished a printed pamphlet in the air. It was a copy of the Carlisle Mortuary Table, and he held it high so the jury could see it.

Death benefit plans are founded on what are known as *mortality tables*. These tables are based on actual statistics, and aim to show the general rate of mortality, and in particular, the rate at each age of life. The Carlisle Table was based on the statistics of two parishes in the town of Carlisle, England. It was compiled from the figures on the census of 1780 and the deaths in the two parishes from 1779 to 1787. Although it tracked only a few lives, the table had proved to be remarkably accurate, and in 1920, it was held in high esteem as a solid reference for determining an individual's probable life span.

"Doctor, are you familiar with the Carlisle Mortuary Table and how it is calculated?"

"Yes, sir. It is the standard table."

"Assuming that Mr. Kennedy was seventy-two years of age in July 1918 when he lost his life and, according to this table, having attained that age, that his expectancy of life was approximately five-and-a-half years, what would you say from your knowledge of his physical condition about whether he would have lived that long or longer?"

"Yes, he would have."

"Dr. McCabe, you have testified that according to the Carlisle Mortuary Table, which has been exhibited and made part of your testimony, Mr. Kennedy's expectancy of life at the age of seventy-two when he was killed was something close to five-and-a-half years. Now, please state, from your knowledge of Mr. Kennedy's health and physical vigor when you last saw him, to what age, barring accident, in your opinion, might he not reasonably have lived?"

"From eight to eight-and-a-half years."

From her front-row seat, Anna Mae Kennedy excitedly reached for her mother's hand. Squeezing it tightly, she let her mother know William McCabe was doing a good job on the witness stand. She squeezed her mother's hand even tighter as Bryan asked the next question.

"Doctor, I believe that you stated you are acquainted with Mrs. Kennedy?"

"Yes, sir."

"Have you treated her as a physician?"

"Yes, sir."

"I will get you to state whether you have seen or treated her recently?"

"Yes, sir."

"Please state to the court and the jury what the condition of her health is at the present time."

"Well, I examined Mrs. Kennedy last Sunday, the 17th, and found her normal in every way except her hearing."

"She is deaf."

"Yes, sir."

"I have no more questions for this witness, Your Honor."

Seth Walker had a short list of questions to ask Dr. McCabe, and he briskly stepped up to the stand. "Dr. McCabe, you didn't ever examine Mr. Kennedy like you did Mrs. Kennedy?"

"No, sir."

"You never did make an examination of his urine or anything like that?"

"No."

"You never examined him. So, all you know about him is what you saw from general observation?"

"That is right."

As Walker forced McCabe to admit that he had never examined David Kennedy, some of the men of the jury—along with many courtroom spectators—wondered why Mrs. Kennedy's lawyer had not called in David Kennedy's own doctor to testify. It was a valid question, one that was never asked or answered in court.

Dr. Duncan Eve, Jr., was the assistant chief surgeon for the NC&StL Railway, and for years, David Kennedy—like most other longtime company workers—had received his medical treatment at Dr. Eve's office. Dr. Eve had even witnessed firsthand the condition of the engineer's dead body. Late on the night of the accident, he had stopped by the Kennedy apartment to examine the remains.

Seth Walker changed tact in his cross-examination. He steered his questions away from the health of David Kennedy and toward medical problems faced by aged men in general.

"It is a fact that when a man gets to be seventy-two years of age, after having a hard life of manual work, that when his system does commence to go down, it goes fast. Is that correct, Dr. McCabe?"

"Well, there are two periods of a man's life that will frequently kill him," the doctor answered. "One is in his young life when he is subject to infectious diseases like measles, scarlet fever, typhoid fever and things of that kind, and another period is beyond middle life when he becomes susceptible to things like cancer, hypertrophy of the prostate, and diseases of that character, then after he reaches beyond that period that he usually dies from the effects of old age, hardening of the arteries, and hemorrhage of the brain which results from hardening of the arteries and diseases of degeneration."

"These are diseases of the old age?"

"Yes, sir. That is right."

The attorney left the front of the witness stand and moved nearer to the jury. Watching them closely, he made a loud statement for dramatic emphasis. "Mr. Kennedy was seventy-two, I believe." Turning on his heels, he spun around and volleyed the last question he had for Dr. McCabe. "So, he was a little past threescore and ten?"

"Yes, sir he was."

The cross-examination of Dr. William McCabe was over. Judge Neil cried out from the bench, "Court is adjourned until Monday morning!"

Chapter Twenty-Four

Court reconvened on Monday, October 25th, 1920. Railroad Engineer William S. Hailey stood at the front of the courtroom, where he solemnly swore to tell the truth. He sat down in the chair on the witness stand, making himself comfortable, and prepared to answer Mr. Norvell's barrage of questions.

"You are William S. Hailey?"

"Yes, sir."

"Who do you work for? What is your position?"

"I'm an engineer on the NC&StL road."

"How long have you been an engineer, Mr. Hailey? Approximately."

"I've been an engineer since 1911. I started firing in 1902 and became an engineer in 1911, but have gone back to firing several times since becoming an engineer."

"Mr. Hailey, did you ever fire for Mr. Kennedy?"

"Yes, sir."

"When was the last time you fired for him?"

"I think the last time I fired for him was the first half of January of 1918."

"Now, going on back and taking the different times you did fire for him into account, how much did you fire for him altogether?"

"I should judge about four, maybe five years."

"Of course, you knew him pretty well when you were firing for him, after you quit firing with him, and in between times. Did you know him well?"

"I expect when I was firing with him I saw him more than anybody, but after I left him, I would still see him about sometimes."

"You saw him frequently, then?"

"Yes, sir."

Picking up a photograph from a nearby table, Norvell approached the witness stand. Leaning in closely, he showed it to Mr. Hailey.

"This picture is marked Exhibit Number One to Mr. Eubank's testimony," he said as he handed it over. "It purports to show where the wreck occurred." Mr. Novell stood quietly for a moment while the engineer examined the photo. "By the way, Mr. Hailey, did you see the wreck after it happened?"

Looking away from the photo he answered. "Yes, sir. I seen it that afternoon."

"You know where it was, then?"

"Yes, sir."

Taking the photo back from Hailey, Norvell held on to it as he asked his next question. "Do you run on a passenger or a freight train?"

"I run a freight train."

"Did you ever run a passenger?"

"One or two trips, I did."

"But you have run through as a fireman on a passenger train very frequently?"

"Yes, sir."

"Mr. Hailey, I ask if you if it is not only the rule, but also the custom for the engineer to show the fireman his train orders?"

"Oh, yes, sir."

"Is it or is it not then the duty of the fireman to assist the engineer in observance of those train orders by looking out for superior trains?"

"That is what he is shown the orders for. It is the engineer's way to call his attention to what he should be looking for."

"In running a train, what does the engineer generally have to do?"

"You mean how does he take care of it all? The first thing he has to do is to inspect his engine before going out, and oil it, and make sure there is water in the boiler."

"After he starts, then what?"

"Well, before he starts, he has to find out if he has the right to start."

The engineer wasn't answering the question the way Mr. Norvell wanted him to. He patiently repeated himself, trying again. "After he starts, what are his duties then?"

"To keep clear of all superior trains, keep water in the boiler, and keep a lookout ahead."

Frustrated that his witness didn't seem to understand what he was asking him to say, Mr. Norvell rephrased his question. "Does he operate a lever?"

"Yes, sir, he has several levers and airbrakes."

"In regard to ringing the bell and blowing the whistle, does he have any duties there?"

"Yes sir, it is his duty to blow the whistle, and there is an air bell. The bell has a cord to it that runs to the fireman's side and to the engineer's side, too."

"Suppose anything goes wrong with the engine. Not fatal trouble, as you have to stop the engine, but something goes wrong—is it the duty of the engineer to see that it is fixed?"

"To see that it is fixed? Yes, it is his duty to look after repairs, if it is something that can be done on the run. Yes, sir. He must do it, if it can be done."

From her seat across the room, Mary Kennedy stared at the man sitting in the witness stand. She had a keen interest in Mr. Hailey's testimony. Mr. Kennedy had respected the younger railroad man's work abilities and his personal character, and she hoped his testimony would prove favorable to her case. He appeared unflustered, and she hoped that his easy demeanor was a good sign. William Norvell faced her as he moved into her line of vision. She tried to read his lips as he spoke to the witness.

"In running a train, the engineer, we will say, is looking forward, that he is inside the cab. What is in front of him, a glass window? That is what I am getting at."

"Yes, sir. There is glass in front."

"Frequently on those engines there is an armrest on the window that engineers generally keep open by their side?"

"Yes, sir."

"And frequently the engineer is leaning with his head out?"

"Yes, sir."

"Now, Mr. Hailey. The engineer is ordinarily presumed to be on the lookout. That is part of his duty, isn't it?"

"Yes. That is part of his duty."

"If he is engaged in something, say, like trying to fix something, or something else of that kind, what is the duty of the fireman as to being on the lookout?"

"You mean if he is not already on the lookout?"

"Do the rules require that one of them always be on the lookout?"

"Yes, sir."

"The fireman's main duty, I mean his physical, manual duty, is shoveling coal into the engine?"

"Yes, sir. And when he's not doing that, he's supposed to be looking out, too. Both of them; the fireman and the engineer."

"Shoveling coal doesn't take up all his time?"

"No, but it takes up a right smart bit of it."

"He generally shovels a pretty good quantity of coal, closes his fire door, and is on the lookout, is that right?"

"Yes, sir."

"Now, Mr. Hailey, suppose a train is passing with six or seven coaches—and by the way, I will ask you whether or not Number One didn't generally run with six or seven coaches?"

"I don't know the size of the train. From five to seven cars, maybe."

"It's an overnight train, and generally runs with some Pullman cars?"

"Yes, sir."

"Pullman cars are a little heavier than regular coaches?"

"Yes, sir."

"When two trains are passing right on adjoining tracks, an experienced railroad man doesn't have to physically see the number of the engine to tell whether simply an engine has passed him, or whether an engine with five or six coaches and one or two very heavy Pullmans have gone by, does he? Isn't there a certain kind of noise there?"

Throughout the room, onlookers strained their necks to see the reaction. This current line of questioning was crafted to cast aspersions on the testimony of Shorty Eubank, and the curious crowd scanned the rows of people looking for the hapless witness.

Hailey's eyes also scanned the room as he answered. Like the others, he, too, wanted to see where the former conductor was sitting. Spotting him in a seat near the back of the room, Hailey felt sympathy for his one-time fellow worker, and he hesitated before giving his answer.

"Yes, sir, there is a noise the whole time the train is passing. There's quite a difference before the sound of a light train and a heavy one."

"Is it such a difference that even an ordinary layman, not even an experienced railroad man could tell the difference? Is there that much difference in the sound?"

The witness sighed. "Yes, there is."

"Now, Mr. Hailey, is it the responsibility of the engineer to see that superior trains have passed?"

"Sure, it is."

"And what it is the duty of the conductor in that regard?"

"The same as the engineer."

"What is the duty of the flagman, particularly if he knows that the conductor is quite busy, as to ascertaining the passage of superior trains?"

"He is supposed to be on the lookout. It doesn't matter if the conductor is busy or not."

꒰ꜛ꒱

A witness in uniform now took the stand. This time, though, the witness wasn't a railroad man. William P. Johnson had been a personal friend of Kennedy's, and was called solely to testify to his friend's health and wellness. There were rampant public rumors about David Kennedy's eyesight that needed to be addressed and quashed if William Norvell expected to clear his name.

Norvell started off by asking about the man's occupation. "Mr. Johnson, you are on the police force of the City of Nashville?"

"Yes, sir."

"You knew Mr. David Campbell Kennedy for a good many years before his death?"

"Yes, sir."

"How well did you know him, Mr. Johnson? Were you one of his good friends or a casual acquaintance?"

"I knew him intimately."

"Mr. Johnson, at or about the time of his death, what was his ability to get around and to walk and to move?"

"Good."

"To a casual observer, to a man who hadn't known him for years, would he appear to be a man of seventy-two years of age?"

"He didn't get about like a man generally would of that age."

"Did you ever know him to be sick with any serious matters at all?"

"No, sir."

"Was he a man, at that age of life, who was generally on the job and around, or was he a man who laid off frequently?"

"He was always out on the job, as far as I know."

"You were with him frequently, were you not?"

"Frequently. Yes, sir."

"Mr. Johnson, you used to play cards with Mr. Kennedy, did you not, at Mr. Geary's?"

"Yes, sir."

"It was a perfectly lawful game, we will assume?"

"Yes, sir. We used to have a sociable game of euchre. On other occasions, he would come to my house and I would go to his."

"Now, his ability to see the cards was all right, was it? Age hadn't dimmed his ability to see?"

"No, sir. He was a mighty hard man to beat sometimes."

Norvell pivoted to face the bench. "I am through with this witness, Your Honor." He returned to his seat.

Seth Walker rose. There had been much public speculation about David Kennedy's vision since the train wreck had happened. Many people in Nashville believed that the engineer's eyesight had failed him. They believed he took his train out on the mainline because he couldn't read the numbers on the switch engine when it passed by in The Shops train yard, and that he just assumed it was Engine #281 that had passed by.

Mary Kennedy wanted her husband's name cleared of all responsibility for causing the wreck. Norvell's prior line of questioning had been designed to dispel the public notion that the train wreck happened because the engineer's eyesight was weak and had failed him on that fateful morning.

As defense attorney for the railroad, Walker had little patience for that course of reasoning. It was his client's perspective that the engineer didn't follow railroad rules and protocol, and that the engineer was therefore one hundred percent responsible for causing the wreck—failed eyesight or not. With little regard for the testimony given by W.P. Johnson, Mr. Walker conducted his cross-examination from the defense side of the room.

He asked Mr. Johnson a single question. "He could see a jack from a good long way away, could he?"

"Yes, sir. He was a mighty hard man to beat at cards."

Amid the chuckles that erupted throughout the courtroom, Seth Walker spoke to the judge. "I have nothing more to ask of this witness," he said.

⁓

Following a short redirect examination by William Norvell of David Kennedy's son-in law, William Jones—during which Jones identified some photographs designating the exact spot where the accident occurred—the attorney for the plaintiff turned the direct examination of the next witness, Tower Operator J.S. Johnson, over to Bryan.

Ever since details of the accident emerged in the official investigation report, many people outside the railroad community—unfamiliar with railroad parlance and customs—struggled to understand why Mr. Johnson remained free of culpability in causing the accident while blame was so freely placed on Mr. Kennedy and Mr. Eubank. During the investigation, Johnson openly admitted to having set the arms of the signal to proceed—giving Number Four permission to go forward—without confirming that Number One had gone by the tower.

On this morning, many of the spectators in the courtroom were especially interested in hearing Mr. Johnson's testimony. They listened in rapt attention to hear what the tower operator had to say.

"In July or should I say, on July 9, 1918, in whose service or employment were you?" Bryan asked.

Mr. Johnson appeared to be at ease in the witness stand, and he answered with a clear voice. "I was in the employ of the Nashville Terminals, sir."

"Are you still in the employ of that company?"

"Yes, sir."

"What was your particular work on July 9th of that year?"

"I was the tower-man at the NC&StL Shops on July 9th."

"What time of day did you go on duty that day?"

"Well, it was about five or six minutes after seven o'clock in the morning."

"Who gave the signal to proceed? You or your predecessor?"

"I did."

"You got no orders for a stop signal from anyone? Had you received any order about Number One that was due in Nashville about that time?"

"No, sir, I did not."

"You saw Number Four as it passed, did you?"

"Yes, sir."

"And your signal on the tower, at that time, was to proceed?"

"Yes, sir."

"How long have you been in the railroad service, Mr. Johnson?"

"I believe I entered service in 1892, about twenty-seven or twenty-eight years ago."

"You are well versed in railroad rules and customs?"

"Yes, sir."

"Does a passenger train carry a flagman?"

"Yes, sir."

"Where is his place, the flagman on a passenger train?"

"The flagman is supposed to protect the rear of the train, as I understand it."

"Now after Number Four passed, did you report it to anyone or anywhere?"

"I reported to the train dispatcher."

"What was the reply?"

"He said it was supposed to meet Number One there. Then he said, 'Can you stop him?'"

"Did you make an effort to stop Number Four?"

"Yes, sir."

"What did you do?"

"I have an emergency whistle in the tower that works by air. It's an air whistle that we always used for emergency purposes. It's not used for any other purpose, and I caught hold of that whistle and tried to stop the train."

"Was the flagman on the rear of that train that morning? On the rear of Number Four?"

"I didn't see him."

"State how far... was the train in sight when you gave the signal to stop the train?"

"Yes, sir, it was in sight."

"Was it within hearing distance from the tower to the rear of the train?"

"I suppose so."

"Mr. Johnson, other than blowing the emergency whistle, what else, if anything, was done to stop that train by you or anyone else there at that moment?"

"There were some men down on the platform. I remember seeing one of them wave his hat across the track, a stop signal; that is all the kind of a flag they had. I don't remember who they were. I was trying to keep my eye on the train, and saw some parties out there by the track."

"Please tell the court and jury what waving your hat out that way means in railroad parlance. What did it mean when they did that?"

"That meant stop."

"The man on the track, who was he that gave that signal?"

"I don't know who he was, Mr. Bryan. There is always a crowd of men there every morning when these trains go out. I can't tell you who he was; I don't remember. But I do remember that he did that."

"Mr. Johnson, you stated that you reported that Number Four had passed on its way west. Is it the duty of the man in the tower to report the passing of each train?"

"Yes, sir."

"The man that you relieved that morning, when you relieved him, did he tell you that Number One hadn't passed by yet?"

"No, sir."

Concluding his interrogation of the tower-man, Bryan asked one final question. "And you yourself didn't know whether it had passed or not?"

"No, sir. I did not."

⌇

Railroad Defense attorney Seth Walker opened his cross-examination of Mr. Johnson. "You are now, and were on July 9th, 1918, the tower operator at The Shops?"

"Yes, sir."

"How far west is the tower at The Shops from Union Station?"

"I'd judge it to be about two-and-a-half miles."

"What time did you go on duty that morning?"

"I was a little late. I think six or seven minutes late. About seven minutes after seven."

"What time did Number Four pass the tower?"

"She passed by at seven-fifteen."

"When Number Four passed by at seven-fifteen, you entered that up in your book, did you?"

"Yes, sir."

"Now, after you entered the fact that Number Four had passed, you called up the chief dispatcher at Nashville, notifying him of the fact, didn't you?"

"Yes, sir."

"How long did it take you to look at your watch, confirm the time, enter the fact that Number Four had passed in your book, and call up the dispatcher at Nashville? What period of time did that take?"

"That oughtn't have taken more than a minute and a half. I think the train ran by a full length."

"Wouldn't a train run further than a length in that amount of time? A minute and half is pretty long time. Were you just estimating?"

"Yes, that was an estimate. It wasn't that long a time. When a train comes by, I keep my eye on it to see if it's a full train, then when he passes me I enter it on the sheet, and when the telephone is not busy, I report it. If I pick it up and the train dispatcher is using the wire and giving another order, I wait until he gets through; but in this case the train dispatcher wasn't busy. I gave it promptly, and the train went by just as I reported him."

"When you told him that Number Four had passed The Shops, the chief train dispatcher said to you, 'Passed?' and you said, 'Yes, he passed,' and thereupon the dispatcher said, 'Stop him,' didn't he?"

"Yes, sir. 'Can you stop him?' That's what he said."

"All the time, Number Four, while you were having this conversation, was running on down the track in a westerly direction, wasn't it?"

"Yes, sir."

"How fast was Number Four going when it passed The Shops?"

"I don't know for sure, Mr. Walker, say, twenty-five miles an hour. It might have been thirty."

"How long was this train?"

"It was a regular train. I think those regular passenger trains carried six or seven coaches."

"They say coaches are eighty feet long, aren't they?"

"Yes, regular passenger coaches are about that. I expect that's how long they were."

"The engine and the tender, they are about together as long as a coach?"

"Yes, sir. There are some engines out there that are about ninety feet long, but I don't think this engine was that long."

"With six coaches, a tender, and an engine, that would make this train about seven coaches in length?"

"Yes, sir."

"That would be about five hundred and sixty feet. If it was a train length past the tower when you called the chief dispatcher, it was about five hundred and sixty feet away when he told you to stop it?"

"Yes, sir, according to that estimation."

"When the dispatcher told you to try to stop the train, you ran over and sounded the emergency whistle? You did everything you could to stop the train?"

"Undoubtedly, I did."

"Now, after you sounded the whistle, you tried to wave down the train?"

"Yes, sir."

"Then you sent a switch engine down the tracks after Number Four, trying to stop it, didn't you?"

"We started to. We didn't get far with the switch engine. We tried to get it out, but we decided it was best not to undertake it. The switch engine did sound its whistle at Number Four, about a half mile down beyond me, where the switch engine was standing."

"Number Four just kept on going until it was out of sight?"

"Yes, sir. It did."

"Mr. Johnson, when you went on duty that morning, you saw Number Four as you looked down in the direction of Nashville, coming on and approaching The Shops?"

"Yes, sir."

"You gave the signal controlling the movement of Number Four up to The Shops that morning?"

"I guess the block man in the partition before me let Number Four in the block. Then, I gave the signal he should have the right to run through the yards."

A block was a section of railroad track controlled by a signal system. No train could enter or exit the block unless given a signal to proceed, and it was that system of control that Seth Walker referred to when he asked his next question.

"Train Number Four is controlled by a block system, as well as all other trains between The Shops and Union Station, are they not? And were they not, at that time?"

"Yes, sir."

"After they get past The Shops, they are controlled by the superiority of trains, by timetables, and by train orders. And they were at that time. Is that correct?"

"Yes, sir."

"That morning, who gave the signal for Number Four to proceed?"

"I did, sir."

Seth Walker had finally reached the heart of his cross-examination and he shifted his attention from the man sitting in the witness stand to the twelve men of the jury. Catching the eye of one juror, he spoke loudly and clearly as he asked Mr. Johnson the question that would matter most. "You didn't know whether Number One had arrived or not when you gave this signal?"

"No, sir, I didn't know it."

"And, as far as you were concerned in the discharge of your duty, it didn't make any difference whether Number One had gone by or not?"

"No. It didn't matter. Not a particle."

Maintaining eye contact with the juror, Seth Walker spoke again. "You had no right to control the movements of a train by your signals so as to supersede the superiority of trains, or stop a train, or to supersede a train order, or anything like that, did you?"

"Certainly not!"

"So, when Number Four pulled in that morning, you lined up the switches for it?"

"Yes, sir."

"You gave a signal indicating that the signals were thrown for Number Four to move on, provided that he had a train order or had the right to go?"

"Yes, sir. That was it exactly."

"Unless Number Four had the right to proceed past The Shops, the signal that you gave him indicating that the switches were thrown for him meant absolutely nothing to him."

"That is right, sir. The signal meant nothing at all."

Walker turned to the judge. "I have no more questions, Your Honor."

There it was. The answer to the mystery that had puzzled many non-railroaders ever since the investigation report was first released. Mr. Johnson held no fault because the railroads rules and regulations protected him. He was deemed blameless because he followed the rules.

For the rest of the afternoon after Mr. Johnson left the stand, William Norvell and Seth Walker argued before the judge as they re-examined and cross-examined William Jones, Shorty Eubank, Patrick Geary, and Anna Mae Kennedy. Finally, both sides rested, and the case of *Mary Kennedy v the Nashville Chattanooga and Saint Louis Railway* was officially in the hands of the jury.

Chapter Twenty-Five

Late in the day, on Tuesday, October 26th, 1920, the jury returned to the courtroom with their verdict.

Mary Kennedy was present when the jury arrived. She sat in the front row between her daughters, Katie Belle and Anna Mae. Sitting in the courtroom day after day had taken an emotional toll on the family. They let out a collective sigh of relief when the jury filed in. Whatever happened, good or bad, the three women believed that the battle would finally be over.

In order to win a judgment for the plaintiff, her attorneys had had to show negligence by the federal agent running the railroad and the railroad company or one or more of its employees played a part in causing the train wreck. After sitting through three days of testimony, almost everyone who had watched the trial believed that Kennedy's two lawyers had done a good job proving their case. Few were surprised when the jury awarded Mary Kennedy a judgment of eight thousand dollars under the Federal Employers Liability Act.

When the judgment was announced, William Norvell scribbled the figure down on a scrap of paper and passed it over to Mary Kennedy. Although the judgment was equal to the average compensation paid out to the beneficiaries of the other white victims—and more than seven times higher than the eleven-hundred-dollar compensation paid to the beneficiaries of non-white victims—it was much less than what her attorneys had asked for, and the number was disappointing.

Worse, by finding that "other members of the crew as well as the engineer were bound to look out for the approaching train, and that their negligence contributed as a proximate cause to the engineer's death," the jury denied Mary Kennedy what she desired most. Her financial concerns were secondary to the burning need she felt to reclaim her husband's memory.

A shadow fell across her soul as she read the jury's words and realized that even though the jury placed equal blame on Mr. Eubank, Mr. Sinclair and the deceased Fireman Luther Meadows they also included David Kennedy in their charge of negligence.

Every day since that dreadful summer morning back in 1918, she had prayed to clear her husband's name. This lawsuit was supposed to help her do that. Now, the verdict was in, and even though she "won" her suit, she felt no triumph in her victory.

She clutched her chest. Her heart was breaking. Her cherished and departed husband was still—and always would be— known as just The Blunderer. It didn't matter that he'd been a hard-working husband, a loving and devoted father, a frequent contributor to charity, or anything else. He would be remembered as the onetime popular and careful engineer who became negligent and caused the Great Cornfield Meet. History would record his name as someone to blame for the deadliest train wreck ever seen in this country, someone who had killed more than a hundred people in that terrible train wreck at Dutchman's Curve.

Like the lonely train whistle her husband never heard on that tragic July morning, Mary Kennedy cried.

Conclusion

In 1924, U. S. Supreme Court Justice Oliver Wendell Holmes reversed the lower court's decision. He delivered the opinion of the highest court in the land, writing about David Kennedy, "It seems to us a perversion of the statute to allow his representative to recover for an injury directly due to his failure to act as required."

Establishing the legal precedent for deciding similar cases in the future, Justice Holmes thus authored the lasting legacy of the unfortunate railroad engineer.

By the time of the Supreme Court ruling, David Kennedy's oldest daughter, Mary Kennedy Jones, and his youngest daughter, Katie Bell Kennedy Charlton, had already moved away from Nashville. The two sisters settled in Dallas, Texas, with their husbands and children. Kennedy's only son, John George Kennedy, had migrated to Ohio in 1919.

Only Kennedy's widow Mary, and his daughter Anna Mae, remained in Nashville. Employed as housekeepers, the two women were cut off both from the benefits the railroad company provided and from the community of railroad families that they were once such a part of. They worked hard to survive. They did their best to separate themselves from the terrible event that had changed their lives forever.

For most people living in Nashville, memory of the train wreck at Dutchman's Curve remained strong, especially for those who lived near the wreck site. At the sound of a train whistle in the distance, farmers working in nearby fields would often stop what they were doing. Straining their ears, they listened closely and held their breath, fearing the sound of another train approaching from the opposite direction. Hats in hand, they would often pause and wait for the oncoming train to safely pass under the bridge.

The concrete white bridge that spanned the railroad tracks was a constant reminder of the railroad disaster. Once called "the new bridge" by locals, they started calling it "the wreck bridge." Soon after the disaster happened curiosity-seekers, would visit the bridge just to stand on it, look down, see the spot where the head on collision had happened, and scrutinize the place where so many people had suffered and died.

But the most vivid reminder of all was the almost-daily sight of Locomotive #281 roaring through Dutchman's Curve. Reported in the newspaper as demolished, the locomotive was actually rebuilt by mechanics at The Shops, as was Locomotive #282. Put back to work in passenger service within the year, the rebuilt #281 operated over the same set of tracks it was running on that fateful day at Dutchman's Curve.

Promoting the slogan "Safety First," officials of the NC&StL Railway Company worked to improve employee and passenger safety on their line. In 1924 alone, nearly six thousand safety operations suggestions were submitted and responded to by the company.

Two years earlier, in 1922, a total of 5,841 people were killed by trains in the United States of America. Of those, 1,794 were killed in highway-crossing accidents, and 2,289 were trespassers on the rails themselves. Another 472 people were killed while getting on or off cars.

Though any loss is terrible for those involved—and even one death is a death too many—the numbers of these types of accidents far outweighed the railroad death accidents that could be reasonably attributed to the operational fault of railroad companies themselves. Collisions and derailments caused less than ten percent of the total railroad deaths that year. Eleven NC&StL trainmen were listed among the 5,841 fatalities that year. (A number of deaths that was far less than the number of employees killed in 1918, when twenty-four NC&StL employees died in the head-on collision at Dutchman's Curve.)

The fact of the matter was that railroad travel was relatively safe, statistically speaking. But of course, things could always be improved—and after such a public disaster, safety was a grave concern and top priority to those involved at every level of the railway industry.

Addressing his fellow employees at the NC&StL Spring Safety Meeting, longtime Conductor H.E. Butler told the assembled workers, "Many things have been done to reduce the hazard, but there still remain dangers incident to the conducting of our country's internal commerce and travel that cannot be eliminated and must depend upon the faithful zeal and intelligent service of the men who in any way contribute to the movement of trains."

Before the meeting was over, Conductor Butler went on to speak in behalf of railroad families. "The words 'Safety First' are more important than may be realized," he said. "In many instances, a failure to fully realize their importance may affect employees' families and cause many unnecessary privations and sorrows that would not have to be borne, if only these words were more prominently in mind while on duty."

By the end of 1924, the NC&StL railway line had replaced its old wooden passenger cars on all fast trains with new, all-steel passenger cars. It was only proper that among the first through-trains assigned new steel cars were the trains on the Nashville to Memphis and Hickman, Kentucky, runs—the same trains that ran over the set of tracks at Dutchman's Curve.

Eight years after the train wreck, in 1926, the NC&StL began installing automatic signals on the line. The signals controlled train movement up and down the tracks, completely preventing the possibility of two trains traveling toward each other from occupying the same set of tracks.

In 1936, the Interstate Commerce Commission issued a statement to the press which read, "In the twenty-seven years this commission has been in existence, the July 9th, 1918, head-on collision near Nashville on the Nashville Chattanooga and St. Louis Railway line is the worst rail disaster, in terms of people killed, this commission has ever had cause to investigate." The statement went on to applaud the railroad company, acknowledging its commitment to the safety and wellbeing of its employees and passengers, by announcing, "It is the determination of this commission that the Nashville-Chattanooga is now the safest railroad company of its class in the country."

Time went by, and the NC&StL kept safety in the forefront. Good fruit was born. In 1942, the railway answered a government challenge for improved safety measures through modernization. Plans to phase out steam engines and dieselize the line were put into action. Diesel engines were much safer to operate than steam engines and Nashville's railroad soon occupied first place among railroads its size in accident ratio of million man-hours worked.

As the decade rolled on, the once-common sight of steam locomotives rolling down the tracks began to slowly disappear in Nashville. After many years of service, Locomotive #281 was finally taken off the road in 1947 and scrapped.

In August of 1948, in a house just ten blocks from Union Station, Mary Kennedy quietly passed away at the age of eighty-seven. For almost nine decades, steam-powered locomotives had provided her life with romance, security, drama, and lonesomeness. Now, as steam locomotives faded into history, it seemed fitting to their legacy that Mary Kennedy, a woman whose life had been irrevocably altered by the collision of two steam locomotives, would fade away, too.

After the wreck, David Kennedy's Locomotive, #282 had been put to work in the NC&StL train yard in Atlanta, Georgia. But the scrap pile beckoned for it, too, soon after Mary's death, and one day the aged machine just vanished from the yard where it had toiled for so long.

No railroad poems, sayings, or superstitions about the two locomotives that crashed together at Dutchman's Curve have ever been found. Even *cornfield meet*, the colloquial expression for a railroad head-on collision, was in use long before Engine #281 and Engine #282 slammed into each other. It's as if the story didn't need any added drama; the truth held intensity enough.

History records that Sunday, January 4th, 1953, marked the end of steam transportation on the NC&StL line when Locomotive #406 rolled west through Tennessee. One railroader witnessing the engine steam out of sight said, "The old Baldwin steamer seemed to realize, somehow, that this was her last trip. Never did the smoke billow up from her stack to such heights." Reflecting on days now gone, he recalled the #406 in its heyday and waxed nostalgic on her final fate. "The locomotive was a real beauty in her younger days. Time was, when she had taken her turn with the best of them in moving peace and war time traffic. Now, rusty, dirty, and wheezy, she was relegated to the last steam passenger run on the line."

And so ended the age of steam locomotives. For more than a hundred years, steam power reigned as the dominant force throughout the United States. With might never seen outside of nature, it had signaled the dawn of a brand new age and revolutionized an entire nation. Locomotives had roared across the continent, transporting people and goods with astonishing speed and power. Mountains were moved, and the landscape was changed to create roads for trains to race over.

Now, they are gone. And we who are left can't help but wonder: could *any* man, not just David Kennedy, really be expected to tame such a powerful beast?

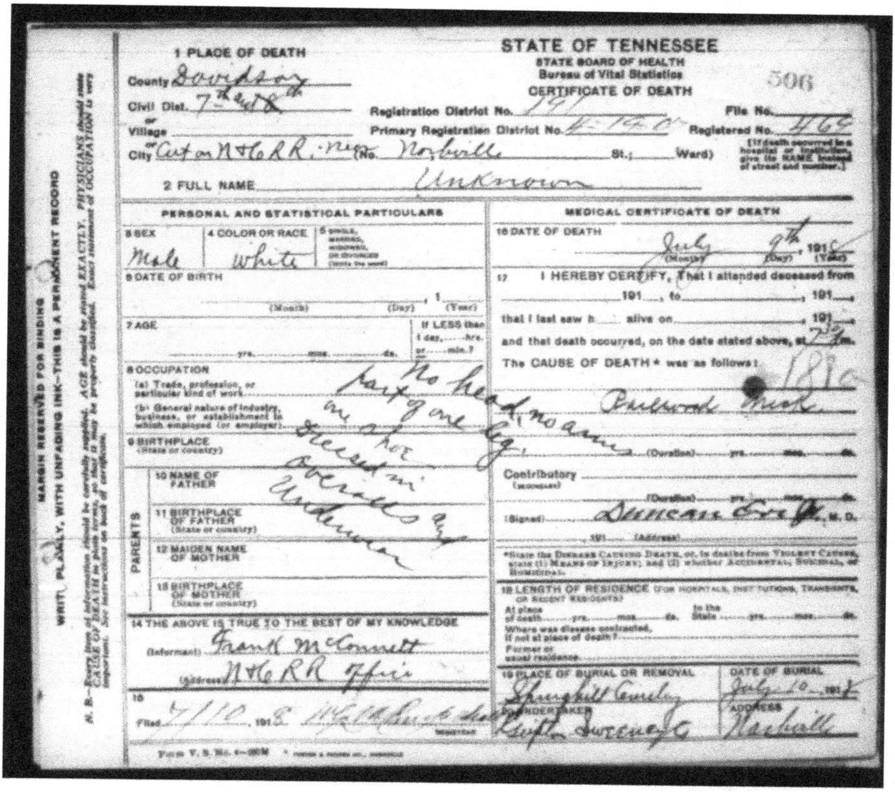

STATE OF TENNESSEE
STATE BOARD OF HEALTH
Bureau of Vital Statistics
CERTIFICATE OF DEATH

506

1 PLACE OF DEATH
County Davidson
Civil Dist. 7th & 8th
Village
City Cut on N&CRR near Nashville St.; Ward)
Registration District No. 191
Primary Registration District No.
File No.
Registered No.

2 FULL NAME Unknown

PERSONAL AND STATISTICAL PARTICULARS

3 SEX Male
4 COLOR OR RACE White
5 SINGLE, MARRIED, WIDOWED, OR DIVORCED
6 DATE OF BIRTH (Month) (Day) (Year)
7 AGE yrs. mos. ds.
8 OCCUPATION
(a) Trade, profession, or particular kind of work
(b) General nature of industry, business, or establishment in which employed (or employer)
9 BIRTHPLACE (State or country)
PARENTS
10 NAME OF FATHER
11 BIRTHPLACE OF FATHER (State or country)
12 MAIDEN NAME OF MOTHER
13 BIRTHPLACE OF MOTHER (State or country)

No head, no arms part of one leg on shoe dressed in overalls and underwear

14 THE ABOVE IS TRUE TO THE BEST OF MY KNOWLEDGE
(Informant) Frank McConnell
(Address) N&CRR Office
15 Filed 7/10, 1918

MEDICAL CERTIFICATE OF DEATH

16 DATE OF DEATH July 9th, 1918
17 I HEREBY CERTIFY, That I attended deceased from 191 , to 191 ,
that I last saw h alive on 191 ,
and that death occurred, on the date stated above, at 7 p.m.
The CAUSE OF DEATH* was as follows:
Railroad wreck
(Duration) yrs. mos. ds.
Contributory (secondary)
(Duration)
(Signed) Duncan Eve M.D.
191 (Address)
*State the Disease Causing Death, or, in deaths from Violent Causes, state (1) Means of Injury; and (2) whether Accidental, Suicidal, or Homicidal.

18 LENGTH OF RESIDENCE (For hospitals, institutions, transients, or recent residents)
At place of death yrs. mos. ds. In the State yrs. mos. ds.
Where was disease contracted, if not at place of death?
Former or usual residence

19 PLACE OF BURIAL OR REMOVAL Springhill Cemetery
DATE OF BURIAL July 10, 1918
20 UNDERTAKER Kirkpatrick Sweeney & Co.
ADDRESS Nashville

WRITE PLAINLY, WITH UNFADING INK—THIS IS A PERMANENT RECORD
MARGIN RESERVED FOR BINDING

AFRICAN-AMERICANS WHO DIED AT DUTCHMAN'S CURVE

Name	Gender	Age	Occupation	Hometown
Unknown	Male	Child		Unknown
Annie Mae Norman Gray	Female	22	Worked At Home	Nashville, Tennessee
Mamie Patton	Female	29	Housekeeper	Nashville, Tennessee
Sallie Walker	Female	30	Unknown	Memphis, Tennessee
Susie Miller	Female	52	Houseworker	Nashville, Tennessee
Unknown	Female		Unknown	Unknown
Unknown	Female		Unknown	Unknown
Unknown	Female		Unknown	Unknown
Unknown	Female		Unknown	Unknown
Unknown	Female		Unknown	Unknown
Unknown	Female		Unknown	Unknown
Unknown	Female		Unknown	Unknown
Arthur Faulkner	Male	17	Unknown	Capleville, Tennessee
Dewitt Cash	Male	17	Laborer, DuPont Powder Plant	Memphis, Tennessee
Mat Toles	Male	19	Laborer, DuPont Powder Plant	Hernandez Mississippi
Marshall White	Male	20	Laborer	Kingston Springs, Tennessee
Oliver Peck	Male	20	Laborer	Craggie Hope, Tennessee
Orville M. Beck	Male	20	Domestic Laborer	Kingston Springs, Tennessee
Johnnie Gordan	Male	21	Laborer, NC&StL Railway	Colesburg, Tennessee
Rodgers Stones	Male	21	Laborer, DuPont Powder Plant	Whitlock, Tennessee

William Lukers	Male	21	Laborer	Helen, Arkansas
Ernest Beck	Male	22	Domestic Laborer	Kingston Springs, Tennessee
Joseph Siempkiest	Male	24	Laborer	Little Rock, Arkansas
Frank Duckett	Male	25	Laborer	Memphis, Tennesseee
W. H. Rogers	Male	25	Laborer, NC&StL Railway	Chattanooga, Tennessee
Jeb Murphy	Male	26	Laborer, NC&StL Railway	Kingston Springs, Tennessee
Jim Hannah	Male	26	Laborer	Pegram Station, Tennessee
Aaron Hicks	Male	30	Laborer	Newsom Station, Tennessee
Frank Hannah	Male	30	Laborer	Pegram Station, Tennessee
Henry Patterson	Male	30	Laborer, NC&StL Railway Shops	Newsom Station, Tennessee
Joe Moss	Male	30	Laborer, NC&StL Railway	Pegram Station, Tennessee
Jack Perry	Male	31	Laborer, NC&StL Railway Shops	Nashville, Tennessee
James Carlton	Male	34	Laborer, DuPont Powder Plant	Memphis, Tennessee
Lonnie Harris	Male	34	Laborer	Memphis, Tennessee
Bess Dunn	Male	35	Laborer, NC&StL Railway Shops	Nashville, Tennessee
Lem Hudson	Male	35	Carpenter, Dupont Powder Plant	Memphis, Tennessee
Will Ferby	Male	37	Laborer, NC&StL Railway Shops	Bellevue, Tennessee
Armer Jones	Male	39	Laborer	Newsom Station, Tennessee
Arthur Robertson	Male	40	Laborer, NC&StL Railway	Kingston Springs, Tennessee
Dan Woodard	Male	40	Laborer	Pegram Station, Tennessee
George Hall	Male	40	Porter, NC&StL Railway	Nashville, Tennessee
George Turner	Male	40	Laborer	Pegram Station, Tennessee

Thomas Reid	Male	40	Laborer	Jackson, Tennessee
James Allen	Male	42	Laborer	Memphis, Tennessee
Jerry Newsome	Male	50	Laborer, NC&StL Railway Shops	Pegram Station, Tennessee
Matt Wilson	Male	50	Switchman, NC&StL Railway	Memphis, Tennessee
Addison Cash	Male	53	Domestic Laborer	Memphis, Tennessee
Dora Lewis	Male	55	Laborer	Kingston Springs, Tennessee
John Patton	Male	57	Laborer	Vaughns Gap, Tennessee
Charles Alexander	Male		Unknown	Unknown
Ed Williams	Male		Unknown	Memphis, Tennessee
Elmer Bell	Male		Unknown	Cumberland Furnace, Tennessee
Frank Harris	Male		Laborer	Arkansas
Griffin Bell	Male		Unknown	Unknown
Joe Woods	Male		Laborer	Unknown
Unknown	Male		Unknown	Unknown
Unknown	Male		Laborer	Kingston Springs, Tennessee
Unknown	Male		Unknown	Unknown
Add Lee Thomas	Male		Unknown	Lucy, Tennessee
Johnnie Whorton, Jr.	Male		Unknown	Memphis, Tennessee
Unknown	Male		Unknown	Unknown
Unknown	Male		Unknown	Unknown
Unknown	Male		Unknown	Unknown
Unknown	Male		Unknown	Unknown
Unknown	Male		Unknown	Unknown
Unknown	Male		Unknown	Unknown
Unknown	Male		Unknown	Unknown
Unknown	Male		Unknown	Unknown

CAUCASIANS WHO DIED AT DUTCHMAN'S CURVE

Name	Gender	Age	Occupation	Hometown
Daniel Timmons	Male	18	Surveyor, NC&StL Railway	Bellevue, Tennessee
Burt Lynch	Male	19	School Teacher	Hohenwald, Tennessee
Wilson B. Harris	Male	20	Unknown	Covington, Tennessee
Newton M. Vanderbrook	Male	21	U.S. Navy Clerk	Jackson, Tennessee
William Scammerhorn	Male	21	Blacksmith	Jackson, Tennessee
F. J. Payne	Male	22	U.S. Navy Recruiter	Covington, Tennessee
Floyd Bell	Male	22	Express Messenger	Waverly, Tennessee
Milton Lowenstein	Male	22	Traveling Hat Salesman	Nashville, Tennessee
Daniel Johnson	Male	25	U.S. Soldier	Chesterfield, Tennessee
Floyd Richard	Male	25	U.S. Navy	Newbern, Tennessee
Lee Purcell	Male	25	Switchman, NC&StL Railway	Nashville, Tennessee
John P. Hussey	Male	26	U.S. Marines Private	Lawrenceville, Illinois
John Kelly, Jr.	Male	30	Fireman, NC&StL Railway	Nashville, Tennessee
John Armor	Male	31	Farmer	Trenton, Tennessee
Joe Jacobs	Male	32	Fireman, NC&StL Railway	Hickman, Kentucky
David William Gardner	Male	33	Superintendent of Water Supply, NC&StL Railway	Nashville, Tennessee
Robert Henry Long	Male	34	Sergeant Police, DuPont Powder Plant	Nashville, Tennessee
Arthur Otto Wolfe	Male	36	Waterwork Department, NC&StL Railway	Nashville, Tennessee

Douglas T. Bates	Male	36	Lawyer	Centerville, Tennessee
John Whitfield	Male	38	Blacksmith	Paducah, Kentucky
Luther Meadows	Male	40	Fireman, NC&StL Railway	Nashville, Tennessee
John Nolan	Male	50	Locomotive Engineer, NC&StL Railway	Nashville, Tennessee
John Herbert Peebles	Male	51	Locomotive Engineer, NC&StL Railway	Nashville, Tennessee
Melville Chadwall	Male	51	Mail Clerk, Railroad Post Office	Nashville, Tennessee
William Knoch	Male	52	Telegraph Operator	Nashville, Tennessee
Alexander Cash	Male	55	Carpenter	Nashville, Tennessee
William Lloyd	Male	63	Locomotive Engineer, NC&StL Railway	Nashville, Tennessee
William Manning Farris, Sr.	Male	67	Merchant	Nashville, Tennessee
David Campbell Kennedy	Male	71	Locomotive Engineer, NC&StL Railway	Nashville, Tennessee
Thomas W. Dickinson	Male	71	Baggage Man, NC&StL Railway	Smyrna, Tennessee
Josiah L. Shaffer	Male	77	Retired Mail Clerk	Nashville, Tennessee
Louis Wood	Male		Unknown	Marvill, Arkansas
Sidney J. Vaughn	Male		Farmer	Louisville, Kentucky
Unknown	Male		Unknown	Unknown
Unknown	Male		Unknown	Unknown

By Paul Clements

Johnson's Lick

The "Sulphur Springs" shown just east of Richland Creek and south of the residence of Charles Bosley on Wilbur F. Foster's 1871 Map of Davidson County, were originally located on land owned by Isaac Johnson, and were known as "Johnson's Lick." The lick was depicted in 1783 and 1784 on plats (Land Records of the Secretary of State of North Carolina, TSLA microfilm #1177, Davidson County files #1039, 1063, and 1383) drawn by Thomas Molloy, and part of that property passed first to William Tait (RODC G-196) and then to Bosley (RODC M-313).

Johnson's Station

The South-Western Monthly (Vol. 1:131-37) contains the information that "Johnson's fort stood on the knoll now occupied by Mr. (Charles) Bosley's house." Bosley's house was shown on W.F. Foster's Map of Davidson County (1871) and Davidson County Chancery Court Plan Book 1, page 93, on the site now occupied by St. Cecilia Academy.

The immediate area surrounding Dutchman's Curve had a long and rich history by the time of the devastating train wreck of 1918. The gently rolling land along Richland Creek had been inhabited for thousands of years before a large prehistoric town was established on the current site of Saint Cecilia Academy and Overbrook School around 1000 AD. By the middle-1400s the entire region had been abandoned in the wake of an apparent collapse of the food supply, and by the mid-1700s the area supported a large population of buffalo, bear, deer, and elk. A small cluster of sulphur springs were located in the general area of Bosley Springs

Road. Because sulphur springs attracted large animals, particularly buffalo, the springs close to Richland Creek were the terminus of five separate prehistoric trails, one of which was eventually supplanted by Harding Road.

European settlement commenced in 1779, and by the mid-1780s Isaac Johnson, the individual who claimed over 1400 acres of the land that included what became Dutchman's Curve, had built a small frontier fort known as Johnson's Station. Although native tribes did not occupy the area when European settlers came into the Cumberland Valley, the entire region was used for hunting by a number of different tribes, and the Indian attacks that had commenced in 1780 would continue across what became Middle Tennessee until 1795.

During those 15 years the settlers were in constant danger of Indian attack. An account of an incident that took place in 1789 was conveyed over a half-century later by an old settler named Hugh Bell, and that account gives the flavor of life on the frontier.

"Captain John Hunter, who had recently married the widow of Mark Robertson, was then living at Bosley's Station. He and I went out in company on January 20 to hunt horses, fearing the Indians would steal them. It was a cold and sleety day. We had gone about three miles. Isaac Johnson had evacuated his weak station at Johnson's Lick, and gone to Brown's.

We were riding along a blind path by the fence side. We had just discovered Bosley's old negro, Sam, some little distance off, throwing corn from a crib in the field into a wagon. This led us to remark, "There's no danger." The first I saw of the Indians, my horse shrank back. I discovered an Indian with his gun leveled, not over fifteen feet distant. A party of about 30 Indians fired upon us. Two balls passed through Hunter's left arm and into his body. He fell dead from his horse.

An Indian fired, not touching me – the smoke rising into my face. Another ball knocked my hat off and grazed the top of my head, making the blood run freely down my long queue. When a volley was fired upon me, my horse instantly wheeled – the loose bridle caught in the end of a fence rail. The horse reared and jumped until he pulled the rail loose – the work of half a minute – and dashed on. I received a ball through my right arm, shattering the bone, and another under the left shoulder blade, passing through my body and up through my left shoulder. A fourth ball made a flesh wound on top of my right shoulder. The firing was one volley, accompanied with deafening yells.

Both arms being helpless, I dropped my loaded rifle, and in dashing off I feared the Indians would shoot me with my and Hunter's rifles. But they probably did not think of it, or perhaps from the signs of blood thought that I would soon drop. The horse took his own course – went three quarters of a mile, where the path forked. The horse took the wrong fork, but seeing his error, made a sudden jump of 15 or 20 feet into the other trail. The suddenness of the jump made the blood fly from my wounds upon the trees, some 10 feet from the ground.

A mile and a half from Johnson's Lick, at Levi Hand's place (near 40th Avenue North and Charlotte Avenue), the horse ran with his head full tilt against the yard gate, and burst it open. He would have dashed into the house had Mr. Hand and family not checked him. They took me from my horse, faint from pain and loss of blood. My hunting shirt was riddled with 17 balls, beside those that had penetrated my body. As soon as the alarm spread, Major Kirkpatrick of Brown's Station (about 100 yards west of the intersection of 23rd Avenue South and Golf Club Lane) raised a party of eight mounted men, put himself at their head, and went in pursuit. They went a mile and a half (near the intersection of Belle Meade Boulevard and Harding Road) and were ambuscaded and fired upon. Kirkpatrick was killed, James Foster and William Brown were wounded – Foster through the left thigh and Brown through the arm and hand."

Later in 1789 there was a second attack, this one on John Cockrill, who ultimately settled on the location of Centennial Park.

"Myself and two more men went out to see if we could see any sign of the Indians, as they had been very much about for several weeks. I was out by (Johnson's Lick), about 70 or 80 yards (from) the other two men. The Indians shot me through the arm and side, but took no bone, and shot my mare as she was wheeling, and threw her on my leg, holding me till they got in about six steps of me. I got loose and rose up with my gun, and killed the nearest one to me. That surprised the others, so I got off and got home."

Additional details of the attack on John Cockrill were related by Charles Bosley who bought the land including Dutchman's Curve in 1817.

"Riding around, Mr. Cockrill was fired upon just at the turn of the creek. One of the Indians ran up, eyeing his foe, laughing in triumph at the fatal predicament he thought Mr. Cockrill was in. His dying horse floundering about, the animal released Mr. Cockrill's leg so as to enable him to seize his gun. Firing on the Indian, he fled for the fort over the ridge, however he fell from the loss of blood before he reached it, and lay in the cane until the next day, but recovered. The Indian fired upon by Mr. Cockrill was so badly wounded that the rest of the party considered the injury mortal. They carried him some distance into the forest, and after building a slight shelter over him, left him to his fate. Whites tracked the wounded Indian for a considerable distance by his blood, but finally lost sight of it. The Indian recovered, and many years afterwards came in and related to the whites the story of his sufferings."

Charles Bosley also knew of a grisly attack that took place on the same property in 1793, 125 years before the train wreck, and very close to the point at which the trains collided.

"Johnson's fort stood about four miles from Nashville. Two boys and two little girls were playing not far off at the spring near the edge of a stream. They were attacked by several Indians lying in wait. One of the girls and one of the boys was killed; the other girl was scalped and tomahawked, and these three were left in a heap upon the ground. The other boy escaped to the fort with a broken arm – the wounded girl recovered."

Bosley made his initial purchase of land in the area in 1817, twenty-two years after the close of the Indian wars. He bought adjoining tracts of land over the decades that followed and his plantation eventually contained over 1000 acres. The sulphur springs, which had formerly been known as Johnson's Lick, became known as Bosley's Spring and was a highly popular outdoor gathering place for the citizens of Nashville wanting to spend a day in the country. Charles Bosley, one of the largest slave owners in the region, still owned the land at the outbreak of the Civil War. The first day of the Battle of Nashville swept across his fields and woodlands, but his house – built on the site of Johnson's Station – survived the fighting.

Bosley died in 1870 and the land passed to his great-granddaughter, Gertrude Bowling, who continued to own the farm well into the twentieth century.

Paul Clements is a Nashville writer and historical researcher. He is the author of Chronicles of the Cumberland.

By Terry Coats

The NC&StL Railway

1845-1957 The Beginnings

The Nashville and Chattanooga Railroad, pre-genitor of the Nashville, Chattanooga and St. Louis Railway, though not the first railroad to charter in the state, was the first to both charter and operate successfully as a railroad company in the state of Tennessee.

In a December 1846 letter to South Carolina Senator John C Calhoun, Vernon K Stevenson, future president of the Nashville and Chattanooga Railroad pointed out to the illustrious politician the importance to the state of South Carolina, the state of Georgia, and especially to the city of Charleston a need for a connecting rail link between the Atlantic Ocean and the Middle Tennessee area.

Stevenson noted the quantity of tobacco, corn, beef cattle, hogs, whiskey, brandy, iron, wool, horses and mules, and cotton produced in Middle Tennessee amounted to over twelve and one half millions of dollars of agricultural and manufactured goods each year. Knowing the importance of having trading partners, Stevenson was at the time soliciting help from the former U.S. Vice President in raising monies to fund the building of a rail line between Nashville and Chattanooga. Already completed by this time were rail lines from Charleston across South Carolina to Augusta, Georgia then from Augusta to Terminus (Atlanta) and then turning north, a line to Chattanooga. The next natural step in this progression was to build a final link to Nashville.

In his letter, Stevenson went on to indicate to Calhoun that if he assisted in acquiring the funds, with the completion of the railroad, the area would surely be able to double its production. Stevenson campaigned the Senator, the city of Charleston, the Tennessee State legislature, the residence of Nashville, and several towns between Nashville and Chattanooga that lay along the path of the proposed rail line.

Within two years, monies were raised; a charter was granted by the Tennessee legislature in 1845, and by April 1851 the N&C had completed laying its first 10 miles of track to Antioch, Tennessee. After tunneling its way though the Cumberland Mountain chain above Cowan the railroad reached Chattanooga in 1854 and there it connected with the rails from Georgia and South Carolina. There was now an open 550-mile long ribbon of iron from Middle Tennessee to the seaports in Charleston and Savannah.

The War Years 1861-1865

The years of the War Between the States were both windfall and disaster for the Nashville and Chattanooga Railroad. The Confederate government used the line to transport men, munitions and materiel for their armies. So lucrative was the business in the early years of the War, it allowed the N&C to pay back to the state of Tennessee much of the debt owed for its initial construction loans. The downside was that as the War progressed both the Confederates and the Federals used the N&C as a primary transportation link. Each army tried its best to destroy the rails and equipment of the railroad when the other army had control of the line. At War's end, the railroad was in shambles, and its locomotives and cars were either destroyed, refugeed off the N&C to keep it safe, or they had been completely depleted from over use. Of 306 cars owned at the start of the War, only 82 were serviceable afterward. The details on the locomotives were worse, of thirty-five in service in 1861, only nine were operable at the end of hostilities. At war's end, the Nashville and Chattanooga reported its losses at $1,891,022.

1868-1896

Enter the savior of the railroad ...Col. Edmund W. Cole. Coleman reached the presidency of the N&C in 1868 and oversaw its reconstruction after the dark years of war. Under his guidance, not only did the railroad overcome its indebtedness but also within a short time, was making moderate profits.

In 1873, the Nashville and Chattanooga Railroad re-chartered to become the Nashville, Chattanooga and St. Louis Railway. Along with the name change came the acquisition of a number of smaller lines across Tennessee, Kentucky, Alabama, and Georgia. Many if not all of these lines unable to repay pre-War loans, had defaulted on those loans, and had been forced into bankruptcy. By 1880, after purchasing several of these bankrupt railroads, the NC&StL had quadrupled in size and was pushing rail tentacles toward St. Louis and Atlanta. The NC&StL was well on its way to becoming the largest and most predominant railroad in the Mid-South.

Not to be outdone and fearing that with the massive expansion of the NC&St.L, the Louisville and Nashville Railroad would be overshadowed as a Mid-South railroad, in 1879 the L&N tried to purchase a controlling portion of NC&StL stock. Acting Louisville and Nashville Railroad President Horatio Newcomb took it upon himself to personally travel to New York City to persuade former Nashville and Chattanooga President Vernon Stevenson to sell his 51% of NC&StL stock. President Cole adamantly fought to keep control of the railroad but it was to no avail. Stevenson sold his controlling holdings and in 1880 the NC&StL would revert to a subsidiary company of the L&N.

Gone were the grand dreams of reaching St. Louis, gone were the plans of becoming the predominant player in the railroad scene.

The hostile take over of the NC&StL did not sit well with the citizens of Nashville. It was said that the L&N would have immediately merged the two companies had it not been for the outrage of the citizens in Nashville who if the merger had gone through threatened to burn L&N depots, bridges, and equipment to the ground. Remembering the carnage inflicted on Yankee troops and equipment during the War by southern partisans, it is thought that the L&N took heed and left things alone. The companies would not merge until 1957.

The 1897 Tennessee Centennial Exposition

Big spectacular worlds fairs or expositions were all the rage in the waning years of the nineteenth century. Fairs in London, Paris, Chicago, and New York had made an indelible impression on the attendees. Seeking to showcase the centennial of the state of Tennessee and in an attempt to reverse the effects of a depression in business in the Nashville area, the NC&StL spearheaded a movement to hold an exposition in Nashville slated for 1896. Plans were developed too late to make the 100th anniversary of the state but under the forceful directions of Major Eugene Lewis and co-chaired by NC&StL President Major John W. Thomas the exposition came to fruition the following year in 1897. The Tennessee Centennial Exposition was a golden opportunity for the NC&StL to transport what would turn out to be over 1.8 million visitors that came to the fair between May and October. Additionally, the NC&StL got to shine as the host of a fair that showcased industry, agriculture, commerce, transportation as well as displays on educational and cultural advances. Highlighted were buildings dedicated to the social progress made by women,

Blacks, and children. The exposition sought to present the New South image of a progressive industrial society replacing that of a rural antebellum.

After the six-month run of the fair most of the exhibition buildings were razed and the grounds were converted into a city park. Centennial Park remains today as the premier jewel in the Nashville parks system.

1890-1918

Trackage rights were obtained from the Illinois Central Railroad in 1899 between Martin, Tennessee and Fulton, Kentucky. Over these tracks the NC&StL routed what would become the queen of all southern trains the "Dixie Flyer." With the inception of the Flyer trains and though it was almost twenty years late, the NC&StL finally could say they were operating trains in and out of St. Louis. This goal had been thwarted with the take over of the NC&StL by the L&N.

Events culminating in the fading years of the 1890 set in motion several key players that would play an instrumental part in the events at Dutchman's Curve on July 9, 1918.

1890 saw the completion of the "New Shops" a 23-acre industrial complex used by the NC&StL for its locomotive repair, blacksmithing, roundhouse, wheel shop, upholstery/paint shop, and car erection shop. It was from the location of The Shops that the Memphis bound train would transfer from double to the single main and would just minutes later be involved in the collision.

In the early 1890's, the NC&StL and the L&N operated jointly a terminal and yard in Nashville at 10th Avenue North and Broadway. In August 1898, they broke ground in that yard for the construction of a new Union Station. Completed in 1900, the Victorian Romanesque Revival station was the dream fulfilled of the same Major Eugene Lewis who had headed up the 1897 Tennessee Centennial

Exposition. From this Union Station the ill-fated passengers of the Memphis bound train departed on this crucial day.

The United States entered WWI in 1917. The government ascertained that the private railroads in the US were incapable of serving the war efforts and therefore in December of that year took it upon themselves to nationalize all railroads under a war powers act. In a move to standardize the railroads, the newly formed United States Railroad Administration established rules that consolidated duplicating routes; labor intensive and costly sleeping cars were dropped from train consists, and terminals, shops, and amenities were closed or consolidated forcing competing railroads to share facilities. Additionally, train schedules were changed supposedly in an attempt to streamline efficiency. It was one of these reconfigured USRA timetables that corralled NC&StL trains #1 and #4 into a tighter operating window. This alteration turned out to be one of the major contributing factors in the accident at Dutchman's Curve.

1919- 1957

The USRA returned control of the railroads to the respective companies on March 1, 1920.

The Golden Age for railroading occurred in the United States in the early years of the 1920's. It was during that decade that the railroads hit a zenith in the amount of track mileage operated and the number of passengers traveling. But, this Golden Age was short lived. Highways improved and automobiles and trucks became more prevalent. Competition from America's highway began to weigh heavily on the railroads. Passenger train travel fell from vogue. Additionally, an increase in power given to the Interstate Commerce Commission after the demise of the USRA resulted in the ICC regulating rate structures involving the rail lines. These regulations of rates were partisan against the railroad and favorable to the trucking industry helping the latter to get a major foothold on controlling freight hauling. These regulations dealt a most damaging blow to rail transportation, both passenger and freight.

The NC&StL, as were most railroads across the country was dealt a devastating financial blow when the Great Depression swept the country. After riding a wave of prosperity in the early to mid 1920's the company was forced to make some deep cost cutting measures in the latter part of the decade. Jobs were eliminated, some branch lines were temporarily shut down, and over 40 miles of track were abandoned. Somehow, the NC&StL was able to stay one step in front of receivership that beckoned at their door though the 1930's.

World War II did bring along a resurgence in passenger travel and the moving of war materiel. American railroads were asked to take on the Herculean task of transporting hundreds of thousands of troops as well of millions of tons of war armaments and supplies.

The US Army chose Middle Tennessee as a major troop training area because the terrain was so similar to that of the European theater. Established were training camps in Nashville, Clarksville and Tullahoma, Tennessee. Two of these camps were located directly on the NC&StL.

The NC was forced to make marked upgrades in tracks, signaling, and equipment to handle the enormous business generated in the war. Tracks and bridges were upgraded, centrally controlled signals were installed, powerful steam locomotives and boxcars were purchased, and new operating procedures were introduced. The railroad was in excellent condition after all the improvements had been introduced.

The NC&StL was always known as one of America's premier railroads. It was the first railroad to offer a pension to its employees, it introduced an 18-week educational training class in conjunction with Vanderbilt University, it was the first railroad to use radiotelegraph to dispatch trains, the first to go intermodal in two areas, operating a ferry service at Hobbs Island, Alabama and bus service on it's Tracy City branch, and was the first railroad in the region to completely dieselize in 1952.

The NC&StL operated as a subsidiary railroad to the Louisville and Nashville after the latter purchased the former in 1890. In 1951 the L&N announced its intention to merge the two roads into one. The merger was granted in 1954 but did not occur for another three year.

On the date of the merger, some jobs were eliminated, others were merged into the parent company, and employee records were transferred from Nashville to L&N headquarters in Louisville. Within a short while the NC&StL logos would be replaced with those of the L&N.

On August 31, 1957, the 112-year old NC&StL did what poet Dylan Thomas warned us not to do and went Gently Into That Good Night.

Terry L. Coats

President- Nashville Chattanooga and St. Louis Railway Preservation Society

Author- Next Stop on GrandPa's Road- History and Architecture of NC&St.L Depots and Terminals.

By Erin Danielle Drake

In the past decade, details about the Great Train Wreck of 1918 have reached unparalleled local recognition. In part due to the historical marker erected in 2008, the availability of online sources, and the fervor of local residents, the wreck has become "mainstream" in many Nashville communities.[1] Betsy Thorpe continues to share the story of the deadliest train wreck in American history through private tours of the site, short informational videos on Youtube, posts on the Dutchman's Curve Facebook Page, and partnerships with local schools. Her creative non-fiction book entitled The Day The Whistles Cried: The Great Cornfield Meet at Dutchman's Curve, is set to be released later this year, becoming the first-full length book on the train crash. In 2010, Thorpe's research inspired songwriters Joel Keller and Marci Salyer to write the song "Dutchman's Curve." Singer and songwriter David Olney released an album that same year with the same title. Though Olney's songs do not explicitly refer to the wreck, they narrate a series of "manageable collisions."[2]

---

[1] Personal Interview, Betsy Thorpe, February 22, 2014.
[2] Edd Hurt, "Rreview of Dutchman's Curve," *Nashville Scene.* Nashville: Tennessee, April 1, 2010. Accessed February 24, 2013. http://www.amazon.com/Dutchmans-Curve-David-Olney/dp/B003F6GQPY

In 2012 southern railroad historian Ralcon Wagner* wrote "America's Deadliest Wreck" for the Trains magazine special "Train Wrecks" edition, providing Dutchman's Curve with an eight-page centerfold. The article is accompanied by a list of "The 20 Deadliest Train Wrecks in the United States" and includes the location, railroad, date, and cause of the wreck. Charts tracking railroad safety improvements and the amount of deaths and injuries of railroad employees over three centuries contextualize the deadly train wrecks by giving the reader a multi-dimensional look at railroads.[3] The developing texts on Dutchman's Curve provide succinct and fascinating information for a new generation of Americans well acquainted with learning about tragedies.

As the wreck approaches its centennial anniversary, the present context of renewed interest is situated within contemporary experiences of disasters. With a multitude of "worst" disasters, occurring in the past fifteen years, the lenses used to assess Dutchman's Curve cannot be separated from the lenses used to assess "natural" disasters such as Hurricane Katrina (2008), the Indian Ocean Earthquake and Tsunami (2004), and the Haitian Earthquake (2010), or "unnatural" disasters like the BP Oil Spill (2010) and the terrorist attacks on 9/11 (2001). Though increased media technology may not allow for the speedy removal of fatal disasters in 2014 as newspapers did in 1918, the current narratives on human suffering in

---

*In the early 1970's Ralcon Wagner attempted to erect a historical marker for the wreck. The Historical Society of Nashville was not interested and the vision for the greenway system and golf course that would eventually spur great interest in the wreck was not in development. Personal Interview, Betsy Thorpe, February 22, 2014.

[3] "Train Wrecks: Derailments That Changed History," *Trains, Special Edition 2012, No. 8-2012*. Waukesha, Wisconsin: Kalmbach Publishing CO.: 2012.

minority and oppressed communities reveal the closeness between Dutchman's Curve and 2014.

In a note on the first page of the Train Wreck special edition magazine, Editor James G. Winn writes, "...one reason why we study train wrecks—to learn from past errors. A derailment is the result of human, natural, or mechanical failures, or combinations of those."[4] As the public reads information surrounding Dutchman's Curve, the magnified social conditions of the Jim Crow South are to be analyzed in tandem with the story of characters like Engineer David Kennedy or Conductor Eubank. Though a revival of sorts, a continued emphasis on the dominant historical narratives of the wreck further masks the reality of everyday structural oppression and unchecked injustices against African Americans and marginalized communities more broadly.

The sources I explored for my project are not the only sources in existence, but the ones accessible via the Internet, the archive, and the newspapers. Many of these objects provide variations of the same details, which allowed me to grasp the technical aspects of the wreck. The lack of archival sources focused on the experiences of black Americans, however, is staggering. It does not imply that the sources do not exist, solely that they do not exist in the archive or dominant sites of historical production. With more research and attention to the black victims, survivors, and descendants, the narrative of the wreck will begin a process of renewal. This renewal will initiate the process for a contemporary reading of Dutchman's Curve not predicated on a narrative of American progress, but instead on an effort to revive the silenced black voices in history.

---

[4] "Why We Study Train Wrecks," *Trains*. Waukesha, Wisconsin: Kalmbach Publishing CO.: 2012, 3.

I came across the story of Dutchman's Curve by chance, and stayed because of the many ironic, paradoxical, and complex social and political factors that converged in my hometown, Nashville, Tennessee. The histories I have read and uncovered represent life in 1918, but also gesture toward other events that have been buried in dominant historical narratives. Further research into the lives of black victims, survivors, and present day descendants is the next step for creating a black countermemory. This memory would focus on the events of Dutchman's Curve, but also continue to ask the questions that were posed in 1918 but went unanswered. The existence of the countermemory makes it possible for future historical narratives not to be derailed by hegemonic forces, but to instead thrive in an effort to coexist at similar values. Until the question, "How long?" is answered, however, attempted revivals will be necessary.

Excerpt from: MORE THAN HUMAN ERROR: BLACK BODIES AND MEMORY IN THE GREAT NASHVILLE TRAIN WRECK OF 1918

By: Erin Danielle Drake

Presented to the

Committee on Degrees in History and Literature in Partial Fulfillment of the Requirements for the Degree Bachelor of Arts with Honors at Harvard University

REPORT OF THE CHIEF OF THE BUREAU OF SAFETY COVERING THE INVESTIGATION OF AN ACCIDENT WHICH OCCURRED ON THE NASHVILLE, CHATTANOOGA & ST. LOUIS RAILWAY AT NASHVILLE, TENN., ON JULY 9, 1918.

AUGUST 16, 1918.

To the Commission:

On July 9, 1918, there was a head-end collision between two passenger trains on the Nashville, Chattanooga & St. Louis Railway at Nashville, Tenn., which resulted in the death of 87 passengers and 14 employees. and the injury of 87 passengers and 14 employees. After investigation the following report is submitted:

That part of the Nashville division of the Nashville, Chattanooga & St. Louis Railway upon which this accident occurred is a single-track line over which trains are operated by time table and train orders, there being no block system in use. Between Nashville and Shops, a distance of 2.5 miles, it is a double-track line, and at Shops there is an interlocking plant which controls all main line switches there. The accident occurred about half way between Shops and Harding, located 2.5 and 6.8 mils, respectively, from the station at Nashville, and within the city limits of Nashville.

The trains involved in this accident are shown on the time table as southbound passenger train No. 1 and northbound passenger train No. 4, but in the vicinity of the point of accident, southbound trains run practically north and northbound trains practically south. Soutbound trains are superior to northbound trains. Train No. 4 is scheduled to leave Nashville at 7 a.m., and train No. 1 is scheduled to arrive at Nashville at 7.10 a.m.

Train No. 1 consisted of locomotive 281, one baggage car and five coached of wooden construction, one Pullman sleeping car of steel construction and one Pullman sleeping car with steel underframe and ends, in the order named, and was in charge of Conductor Tucker and Engineman Lloyd. It was enroute from Memphis to Nashville, being operated over the Louisville & Nashville Railroad from Memphis to McKenzie, and the remainder of the distance over the Nashville, Chattanooga & St. Louis Railway. It left McKenzie at 3 a.m., passed Bellevue, 12.6 miles from Nashville, at 7.09 a.m., 30 minutes late, and at about 7.20 a.m. collided head on with train No. 4 at a point about 4.5 miles from Nashville, while running at a speed estimated at about 50 miles an hour. Fig. 1 is a general view of the wreck.

Train No. 4 consisted of locomotive 282, one combination mail and baggage car, one baggage car and 6 coaches, in the order named and all of wooden construction, and was in charge of Conductor Eubank and Engineman Kennedy. At Nashville the crew received train order No. 29 reading as follows:

No. 4 engine 282, hold main track, meet No. 7, Eng. 215, at Harding. No. 1 has engine 281.

This train left Nashville at 7.07 a.m. 7 minutes late, passed Shops at 7.15 a.m., and collided with train No. 1 at a point about 2 miles beyond Shops while running at a speed estimated to have been about 50 miles an hour.

The engineman and firemen of both trains were killed. Locomotive 281 was derailed on the west side of the track, the boiler being stripped of cab, machinery and appurtenances, and came to rest in an upright position at an angle of about 45 degrees with the track; it is shown in Fig. 3. Its frame and all machinery were practically demolished. The baggage car was completely demolished. The first coach lay crosswise the track, the combination car of train No. 4 being driven into its side near the center and its rear end torn completely end to a depth of 12 or 15 feet. The second coach was derailed and its forward end went down the bank and rested on the front end of boiler of locomotive 281 and its rear and rested on the roadbed on top of the frame and other parts of locomotive 281, its forward end being badly broken and damaged. The third coach remained on the roadbed with its forward end jammed against the rear of the second coach; the rear trucks of this car and the four following cars were not derailed. All of this equipment was on train No. 1 Figs. 2, 3 and 4 are views of the destroyed equipment.

Locomotive 282 was derailed to the east side of the track, the boiler thrown from the frame and entirely stripped of all machinery and appurtenances and stopped about parallel with the track, the entire locomotive except the boiler being demolished, as shown by Fig. 3. The forward half of the combination car was demolished by coming in contact with the first coach of train No. 1. The baggage car was completely telescoped with the first coach to its rear, both cars remaining upright, but were practically destroyed, as shown by Fig 4. The end of the second coach was demolished for a distance of 6 or 8 feet and partially telescoped with the rear end of the coach ahead of it. The three rear cars of train No. 4 were not derailed and only slightly damaged.

Approaching the point of accident from Harding, the track is straight for about 1,800 feet, then there is a 1-degree curve to the right about 2,100 feet long, then a tangent about 1,100 feet long, then a 1-degree curve to the left about 1,300 feet long, then a tangent about 2,000 feet long, then a 2-degree curve to the right about 1,500 feet 2,000 feet long, then a 2-degree curve to the right about 1,500 feet long, the collision occurring about 900 feet in on this curve. The track just described is laid on a fill and a descending grade varying from 0.3 per cent to 0.7 per cent to within about 350 feet of the point of collision. and then the grade is practically level for about 2,000 feet. About 300 feet south of the point of collision, there is an over head highway bridge over the track and just south of the bridge there are heavy woods on the right hand side of the track.

234

Approaching the point of accident from the direction of Shops, the track is straight for approximately 4,000 feet, then there is a 3-degree curve to the left about 2,200 feet long, then a tangent about 1,000 feet long which leads to the 2-degree curve on which the collision occurred. The grade descends from 0.7 per cent to 1.3 per cent to within about 1,650 feet of the point of collision, and is practically level the remainder of the distance. Between Shops and the point of collision there are several cuts, one of which ends about 300 feet before reaching the point of collision, and has a maximum depth of 15 feet. This cut, the overhead highway bridge and the curve upon which the accident occurred made it practically impossible for the enginemen to see approaching trains is indicated by Fig. 5. The weather at the time was clear.

Dispatcher Phillips stated that when he missed train order No. 29 for train No. 4 to meet train No. 7, he added the information that train No. 1 was being hauled by locomotive 281, it being the custom to advise the crew of train No. 4 of the engine number of train No. 1 in this manner to aid then in identifying that train, and also to advise them that that train had not arrived at Shops. He said trains Nos. 1 and 4 are scheduled to pass on the double track between Nashville and Shops, and in case train No. 4 arrived at Shops before train No. 1, train No. 4 is expected to remain at Shops until train No. 1 arrives, unless the crew receives authority to proceed, train No. 1 being the superior train. He said there was no train register at Shops.

Conductor Eubank of train No. 4 stated that before leaving the station at Nashville, he received a train order advising that engine 281 was hauling train No. 1 and he delivered a copy of that order to Engineman Kennedy who read it back to him. He remarked to Engineman Kennedy that "No. 1 must be some late this morning, but I don't believe the mail is going to delay us so he will have to change that meeting point to Vaughns Gap," and from the remarks passed between them he supposed Engineman Kennedy knew their train was liable to be detained at Shops to meet train No. 1. Conductor Eubank stated that he read the train order to the train porter just as his train was leaving the station and shortly thereafter, and while his train was still on the double track, he delivered the order to the flagman and told him to look out for train No. 1. He said he knew train No. 1 had not arrived at Shops when he left Nashville and kept that train in mind. He was busy collecting tickets and before reaching the end of the double track, he heard a train pass his train on the opposite track, which he assumed was train No. 1, although he could not see it on account of the car in which he was riding being crowded. He said it took all his time and attention to collect the tickets before the next regular stop, and he was depending upon the engineman, fireman, porter and flagman to look out for train No. 1, as was his custom, and stop at Shops in case they did not pass that train. He stated that his train was running at a speed of about 45 miles an hour when he felt the application of the air brakes, followed immediately by the collision. He said he considered Engineman Kennedy careful man of good habits and when talking to him before leaving Nashville, he was apparently in good spirits and normal condition.

Flagman St. Clair of train No. 4 stated that when his train left Nashville, he was riding on the rear end and when it reached Shops he went forward, asked Conductor Eubank for the train orders, received them, but the conductor said nothing to him about looking out for train No. 1. He said a switch engine with 8 or 10 cars passed his train between Nashville and Shops, moving in the opposite direction, but saw no other trains. He said he had made but two trips as a flagman on a freight train, and this was his first trip as a passenger train flagman.

Conductor Tucker of train No. 1 stated that his train was running about 30 minutes late, and at a speed of 50 or 60 miles an hour, when the collision occurred, but he felt no application of the air brakes. He said he had received no orders concerning train No. 4, but it being an interior train, he expected it to wait at Shops until his train arrived.

Conductor Riggle, who alternated with Conductor Eubank on train No. 4, stated that he always kept train No. 1 in mind after leaving Nashville, and made it a special point not to pass Shops unless he personally knew that that train had arrived; on several occasions he had waited Shops until that train arrived. He said he depended upon the flagman, porter, and engine crew to identify train No. 1, but would not permit his train to pass Shops unless they advised him it had arrived, or he saw it.

Engineman Winford, who alternated with Engineman Kennedy on train No. 4, stated that it was sometimes necessary to wait at Shops until train No. 1 arrived. He said he usually finds the signals at Shops set for movement to the single track, but he always waited until the arrival of train No. 1, it being his understanding that the interlocking signals gave his train to rights over superior trains beyond Shops.

Operator Johnson stated that he went on duty at Shops at about 7.06 a.m. or 7.07 a.m., and train No. 4 passed the tower there about 7.15 a.m. at a speed of about 25 miles an hour. At that time he did not know whether train No. 1 had arrived, and did not examine the train sheet to see if it had; the first notice he had of its nonarrival was when he saw it was not entered on the train sheet. He said he reported the passage of train No. 4 promptly to the dispatcher, who told him to try and stop that train, as it should have waited for train No. 1, and he sounded the emergency air whistle in an effort to attract the attention of the crew of that train, which was then about a train length away, but the signal was not heeded. When train No. 4 approached the tower, the signal was in the proceed position, but he said that did not give it a right to proceed against train No. 1. He said nothing was said about train No. 1 when he took charge of the tower that morning.

Traveling Engineer Fahey stated that he considered Engineman Kennedy a very careful man, well posted on the rules, and one who adhered strictly to them. He said he bad observed engineman passing Shops upon the operator's word that superior trains had arrived, and as a result, the superintendent issued bulletin No. 1268 under date of May 28, 1918, reading as follows:

Understand some engineers on outbound trains are passing the Shops without any definite information as to whether superior trains have arrived, other than to ask operator at Shop tower. This must be discontinued.

Superior trains must either he registered before the northbound train depart or be identified by some member of the crew of the superior train, meet the superior train between Nashville and the Shops or have an order at the Shops stating that the superior has arrived.

NOTE. -- See that train dispatchers understand this and have the orders ready at the Shops so they can be handed on to the outbound trains.

This accident was caused by train No. 4 occupying the main track on the time of a superior train, for which Engineman Kennedy and Conductor Eubank were responsible.

Rule 83 of the operating rules of the Nashville, Chattanooga & St. Louis Railway provides in part as follows:

A train must not leave its initial station or any division, or a junction or pass from double to single track, until it has been ascertained whether all trains due which are superior or of the some class, have arrived or left.

The evidence indicates that Engineman Kennedy and Conductor Eubank had been running on train No. 4 for several years and before leaving Nashville on the morning of the accident they had talked about train No. 1 and knew that it had not arrived, although it was due there at 7.10 a.m., three minutes after their train departed. As Engineman Kennedy was killed in the collision, no evidence could be secured to determine what caused him to overlook train No. 1.

Conductor Eubank apparently relied wholly upon the other members of the train crew to identify train No. 1 and allowed his train to pass from double track to single track at Shops without making any effort to ascertain whether train No. 1 had arrived. His statement that he was busy collecting tickets and that he passed a train in the yards between Nashville and Shops, which he did not see, but assumed was train No. 1, can not be considered a valid reason for overlooking of failing to identify that train. His first duty was to provide for the safety of his train and see to it that it did not pass from double track to single track before train No. 1 had arrived; and particularly in a yard where switching movements are constantly being made, he was extremely negligent in assuming that a passing train was No. 1 without seeing it and without being notified of its identify by some member of his crew who had seen it.

While the operating rules of the company required that a train must not pass from double to single track "until it has been ascertained whether all trains due, which are superior, or of the same class, have arrived or left," no means were provided by the company to enable employees to secure definite information of that character. That responsible operating officers were well aware of the conditions existing at Shops, as well as the fact that train employees were not strictly adhering to the requirements of the rule, is evidenced by the superintendent's bulletin No. 1268, issued last May. It appears that bulletin contemplated orders would be issued and delivered to outbound trains at Shops giving notice of superior trains which had arrived, but no practice of this nature was in effect. The custom of merely notifying outbound train crews of the number of the locomotive hauling an opposing superior train was utterly inadequate as a safeguard, for under the practices followed, the train crew was required to observe and correctly read the number of the passing locomotive under all conditions of weather and traffic.

The records show that during the month of June, on average of 23 trains daily were operated into and from

Nashville over this division, and the number of yard movements materially increased the density of traffic between Nashville and Shops.

Under these circumstances, it is absolutely essential to safety that some means be provided for supplying to outbound crews definite information regarding opposing superior trains, as, for example, by the maintenance of a train register at Shops, or by issuing orders to outbound trains at Shops giving definite notice of the arrival at that point of superior trains which had not arrived at Nashville at the time of departure of the outbound trains.

This accident would have been prevented, beyond question of doubt, by a properly operated manual block system on the single-track line north of Shops, for which all necessary appliances and facilities were already available. The time table indicates that between Nashville and Hickman, Ky., a distance of approximately 172 miles, there are 27 train-order offices, of which 14 are continuously operated. On this line there are 4 schedules passenger train in each direction, and a total of 12 schedules freight trains. With this volume of traffic, and in view of the universally recognized features of increased safety afforded by the block system, there can be no valid excuse for the failure or neglect on the part of the railroad company to utilize existing facilities for the purpose of operating a block system on that line.

It is to be noted that all the cars of both trains, except the two sleeping cars on train No. 1, were of wooden construction, and six of these wooden cars were entirely destroyed. This accident presents a more appalling record of deaths and injuries than any other accident investigated by the Commission since the ancient-investigation work was begun in 1912. Had steel cars been used in these trains, the toll of human lives taken in this accident would undoubtedly have been very much less.

All of the employees involved were experienced men, with the exception of the flagman, with good records, and at the time of the accident the crew of train No. 4 had been on duty 52 minutes, and the crew of Train No. 1, 9 hours and 52 minutes.

Respectfully submitted.

W. P. BORLAND,

Chief, Bureau of Safety

Appendix F: Supreme Court Decision

JAMES C. DAVIS, AGENT, v. MRS. MARY KENNEDY,
ADMINISTRATRIX, ETC.
No. 371.
SUPREME COURT OF THE UNITED STATES
263 U.S. 692; 44 S. Ct. 6; 68 L. Ed. 509; 1923 U.S. LEXIS 2964
October 8, 1923

COUNSEL:[*1] Mr. Fitzgerald Hall and Mr. Frank Slemons for petitioner. Mr. F. M. Bass and Mr. W. E. Norvell, Jr., for respondent.

OPINION
Petition for a writ of certiorari to the Supreme Court of the State of Tennessee granted.

DAVIS, AGENT, *v.* KENNEDY, ADMINISTRATRIX OF
KENNEDY, DECEASED
No. 85
SUPREME COURT OF THE UNITED STATES
266 U.S. 147; 45 S. Ct. 33; 69 L. Ed. 212; 1924 U.S. LEXIS 2902
Argued October 17, 1924
November 17, 1924

PRIOR HISTORY:[1]** CERTIORARI TO THE SUPREME COURT OF THE STATE OF TENNESSEE
LAWYERS' EDITION HEADNOTES:
Master and servant -- no recovery for death due to employee's own negligence. --
Headnote: No recovery can be had under the Federal Employers' Liability Act for death of a railroad **engineer** who runs his train out onto the main track before knowing that a train from the opposite direction had passed, though he had been asked by the conductor to look out for such train because the train which he was operating was crowded, on the theory that the other members of the crew were bound to look out for the approaching train, and that their negligence contributed in a proximate way to the death of the **engineer.**

242

SYLLABUS

Where a railway collision, killing an **engineer**, was directly due to neglect of his personal duty not to move his train forward without positively ascertaining that another train had passed, the possibility that the accident might have been prevented but for contributory negligence of other members of the crew in not performing the look-out duty devolving also upon them, will not sustain an action by his representative against the carrier under the Federal Employers' Liability Act. P. 148.

Reversed.

CERTIORARI to a judgment of the Supreme Court of Tennessee affirming a judgment for death by personal injuries, recovered under the Federal Employers' Liability Act.

COUNSEL: *Mr. Fitzgerald Hall*, with whom *Mr. Frank Slemons* and *Mr. Seth M. Walker* were on the brief, for petitioner.

Mr. W. E. Norvell, Jr., for respondent.

JUDGES: Taft, McKenna, Holmes, Van De Vanter, McReynolds, Brandeis, Sutherland, Butler, Sanford

OPINION BY: HOLMES

OPINION

[*148] MR. JUSTICE HOLMES delivered the opinion of the Court.

This is an action under the Employers' Liability Act of April 22, 1908, c. 149, § 1, 35 Stat. 65, brought [**2] by the administratrix of David **Kennedy** to recover damages for his death upon a railroad while under federal control. The death was caused by a collision between two trains called No. 1 and No. 4, west of a point known as Shops which was two and a half miles west of Nashville, Tennessee. The tracks were double from Nashville to Shops but after that the track was single. No. 1, bound for Nashville, had the right of way, and the crew of No. 4, bound westward, had instructions never to pass Shops unless they knew as a fact that No. 1 had passed it. **Kennedy** was the **engineer** of No. 4. The conductor had told him that the train was crowded and had asked him to look out for No. 1, which **Kennedy** agreed to do. He ran his train on beyond Shops however and the collision occurred.

The trial was in a Court of the State of Tennessee, and the plaintiff got a judgment which was sustained by the Supreme Court of the State on the ground that the other members of the crew as well as the **engineer** were bound to look out for the approaching train and that their negligence contributed as a proximate cause to the **engineer's** death. We are of opinion that this was error. It was the personal duty of [**3] the **engineer** positively to ascertain whether the other train had passed. His duty was primary as he had physical control of No. 4, and was managing its course. It seems to us a perversion of the statute to allow his representative to recover for an injury [*149] directly due to his failure to act as required on the ground that possibly it might have been prevented if those in secondary relation to the movement had done more. *Frese v. Chicago, Burlington & Quincy R.R. Co., 263 U.S. 1, 3.*

Judgment reversed.

243

Primary Original Material:

Broadbelt Collection of the Baldwin Locomotive Works, 1880-1940, Railroad Museum of Pennsylvania Library and Archives.

Brotherhood of Sleeping Car Porters Collection, Special Collections, Fisk University.

David Kennedy Pension Record, Civil War Pension Papers, National Archives and Records Administration.

DAVIS, AGENT, *v.* KENNEDY, ADMINISTRATRIX OF KENNEDY, DECEASED, Records of the U.S. Supreme Court of the United States, 267.3 1790-1997.

Edgefield/East Nashville Oral History 1977-1978, Nashville Public Library: Special Collections Division.

George E. Haynes Collection, Correspondence, Box Two and Box Four, Special Collections, Fisk University.

Historic Nashville 1980 Oral History, Nashville Public Library: Special Collections Division.

Interstate Commerce Commission Map Collection, National Archives.

Journals of Harry C Monk, part of the Carrie Mae Weil Ornithological Collection, Nashville Public Library: Special Collections Division.

Last Will and Testament of David Campbell Kennedy, Last Will and Testament of William F Lloyd, Documents, Wills, Metropolitan Nashville, Davidson County, Archives.

Mary Kennedy Versus the NC&StL Railway 1922, Middle Tennessee Supreme Court Case Transcript, Tennessee State Library and Archives.

Papers of Bishop Thomas Sebastian Byrne, Correspondence with Monsignor Dennis Murphy, Archives of the Roman Catholic Diocese of Nashville.

Record Group 125 – County Road Petitions – 1911-1965, Metropolitan Nashville, Davidson County, Archives.

REPORT OF THE CHIEF OF THE BUREAU OF SAFETY COVERING THE INVESTIGATION OF AN ACCIDENT WHICH OCCURRED ON THE NASHVILLE, CHATTANOOGA & ST. LOUIS RAILWAY AT NASHVILLE, TENN., ON JULY 9, 1918, Investigations of Railroad Accidents 1911 – 1993, Special Collections, National Department of Transportation Archives.

Tennessee Death Records Tennessee, Davidson County, July, 1918, September 1918, October, 1918, August, 1948,Tennessee State Library and Archives.

Vital Records, Marriage Records of Davidson County, Metropolitan Nashville, Davidson County, Archives.

Books and Magazines:

Bulletin Nashville Chattanooga and St. Louis Railway: n. page. Print. 1924-1954.

Burt, Jesse Clifton. *The Dixie Line*: story of the Nashville and Chattanooga Railroad Company/Nashville, Chattanooga and St. Louis Railway Company, and their relation to each other and to their work forces ; to their communities and to the state of Tennessee; to other railroads, especially the Western and Atlantic Railroad, of Georgia, and the Louisville and Nashville. PHD dissertation, Vanderbilt University, part of the BURT, Jr., JESSE C. (1921-1976) PAPERS 1920-1981 Tennessee State Library and Archives.

Coats, Terry L.. *Next stop on Grandpa's Road*: history & architecture of NC&St.L railway depots and terminals. Nashville, Tenn.: Author's Corner, 2009.

Department of Labor, The negro at work during the World War and during reconstruction Statistics, problems, and policies relating to the greater industry and agriculture. Second study on negro labor..:, 1921.

Kelley, Sarah Foster. *West Nashville-- its people and environs*. Nashville, Tenn.: S.F. Kelley, 1987.

Lovett, Bobby L.. *The African-American history of Nashville, Tennessee, 1780-1930*: elites and dilemmas. Fayetteville: University of Arkansas Press, 1999.

Merritt, Dixon Lanier. *Sons of Martha*; a historical and biographical record covering a century of American achievement by an organization of master builders,. New York city: Mason and Hanger company, inc., 1928.

Nashville City Directories 1863-1948.

Sherman, Joe. *A thousand voices: the story of Nashville's Union Station*. Nashville, Tenn.: Rutledge Hill Press, 1987.

Live Interviews:

Alfred Farris, grandson of Nashville businessman and train wreck victim, Willis Farris.

Brownie Spicer—one of the last living NC&StL steam locomotive engineers.

Chip Curley—son of Julius Curley, who on the morning his tenth birthday, witnessed the carnage of the train wreck.

Denise Nolan Delurgio, granddaughter of NC&StL locomotive engineer and train wreck victim, John Nolan.

Douglas T Bates III, grandson of Tennessee lawyer and train wreck victim, Douglas T Bates.

Dr. Bobby Lovett, senior Professor of History, formerly Dean of the College of Arts and Sciences at Tennessee State University and author of books relating the history of Nashville's African American community.

Duncan Eve III—son of NC&StL railroad surgeon, Doctor Duncan Eve Jr.

Elizabeth Jacobs—last known living witness to train wreck at Dutchman's Curve.

Joe Loftis—great grandson of Henry Clay Loftis, one of the Shops workers who marched out to the train wreck site.

John Egerton, Historian of Southern Culture and author known for his book on the Civil Rights movement.

Kathryn Stoner, niece of NC&Stl railroad man and train wreck victim, Daniel Timmons.

Mark Womack—one time Agent Operator and Chief Head Rules Examiner for the NC&StL Railway.

Pat Nolan of Leesburg Virginia, grandson of NC&StL locomotive engineer and train wreck victim, John Nolan.

Pat Nolan, of Nashville Tennessee, relative of NC&StL locomotive engineer and train wreck victim, John Nolan.

Ridley Wills II, Nashville Historian and author of several books pertaining to the social and economic past of Davidson County.

Robert White—son of NC&StL railroad man, and train wreck survivor Wesley White.

Sue Kennedy Gross, granddaughter of NC&StL locomotive engineer and train wreck victim, David Kennedy.

Terry Coats, Railroad historian, President Nashville Chattanooga Preservation Society and author of a book on the history and architecture of the NC&StL Railway.

Newspapers:

The Chicago Defender
The Nashville American
The Nashville Banner
The Nashville Globe
The New York Times
The Tennessean
The Washington Post

Website:

Bridgehunters.com

About the Author

Betsy Thorpe studied folklore and ethnic anthropology at the University of Oregon and is a scholar of early twentieth-century Southern culture and history. She studied the art of writing creative nonfiction in an online class offered by the Creative Nonfiction Foundation of Pittsburgh, Pennsylvania. A freelance writer, Betsy specializes in reflections on historic and current events. She is also a long-time waitress. She lives with her daughter and three granddaughters in Nashville, Tennessee.

Thorpe is an honorary member of the Bellevue Harpeth Historical Association and the Nashville, Chattanooga Preservation Society. She is also a member of Nashville Historic, Inc. In 2009, she joined the Nashville Writers Meetup Group. She is most proud of her awards in 2011 and 2012 of a private, individual Writer's Room at the Nashville Public Library, an honor bestowed by the library upon a select number of authors. In 2014, Betsy was again honored when she was invited to contribute to the *Nashville Encyclopedia*. This on-line project is creating an important resource documenting Nashville history and culture.

When Betsy is not writing, serving food to customers, or daydreaming about the past, she and her three grand-daughters enjoy watching primetime soaps and crime shows on TV, bicycle riding, cooking Rachael Ray 30-Minute-Meals, and taking Greyhound Bus and Amtrak Train adventures together.

The Day The Whistles Cried: The Great Cornfield Meet at Dutchman's Curve is her first book.

CPSIA information can be obtained
at www.ICGtesting.com
Printed in the USA
LVHW08s2351080718
583118LV00001B/167/P